FOCUS ON THE FAMILY®

BEDTIME Bible

Stories to open young hearts to God's Word

TYNDALE

Tyndale House Publishers, Wheaton, Illinois

Heritage Builders®

BEDTIME Bible

Stories to open young hearts to God's Word

By
Rick Osborne
Mary Guenther
K. Christie Bowler

Illustrated by A. Patricia Jaster

Library of Congress Cataloging-in-Publication Data

A Focus on the Family book published by Tyndale House
Publishers, Wheaton, Illinois.

For Lightwave:
Concept Design and Direction: Rick Osborne
Text Director: K. Christie Bowler
Illustrator: Patricia Jaster
Desktop: Andrew Jaster

Scripture portions taken from the Holy Bible, New International
Reader's Version Copyright © 1994, 1996 by International Bible
Society.

Cover Design: Candi Park D'Agnese

Printed in the United States of America
00 01 02 03 04 05/10 9 8 7 6 5 4 3 2 1

CONTENTS

HOW TO USE THIS BOOK

A Bible with a Difference

My *Bedtime Bible* is designed for you to read with your children. The individual stories, complete in themselves, together form One Big Story: God's plan for the world. It begins with creation and the Fall and progresses through time, as God works to make things right between Himself and humanity. God chose one man, Abraham, and made him into a nation. He guided that nation, His people, teaching them His ways and keeping them safe. From them, God chose a family line (David's) and watched over them. When the time was right, God chose a woman (Mary) and sent Jesus, His Son, to live among us. The Big Story continues through Jesus' life, ministry, death, resurrection, and return to heaven—the climax of God's plan to return us to Himself—and continues on through the spreading of God's good news around the world until the final celebration of heaven itself.

You can read the stories individually and in any order. But if you read them in order, God's plan unfolds through biblical history and His One Big Story will become clear to your children. They will come to know God's heart and love and see what happens when people follow God, as well as when they don't. By the end of the book and your discussions together, your children will know all the basic truths about God, Jesus, salvation, and the Bible that children this age are capable of grasping as outlined in Focus on the

Family's *Guide to the Spiritual Growth of Children.*

The stories in this book are drawn directly from the Bible and wherever possible, we have quoted actual scripture. However, parents should be aware that we have done a certain amount of dramatization. We have sometimes added realistic, colorful details to enhance the understanding of the story, but never at the expense of scripture's original intent.

Then What?

Two questions follow each of the stories to help your children get the most out of it. The first question focuses on the story you just read to help the child think more deeply about what happened. The second generally focuses on some kind of application—the "now what?" of the story.

Following the questions are sample suggestions for prayer. Don't feel limited to these or obligated to use them. Your children might not be ready for that particular prayer. The prayers are simply starting points for you to use before moving on to other prayers. Do make the prayers as concrete and specific as possible, relating them to what your children have just read and, especially, to their lives.

Enjoy!

Engage your children's imaginations as they try to picture what it would have been like to be in the story they're hearing. If you use actions or different voices, you will make the stories come alive. That way, your children can see and feel the reality of the Bible, the closeness of God, the awfulness of sin, and the wonder of God's love and power.

As you read, your children will listen and look at pictures. Hidden somewhere in each picture is a mouse. Encourage your children to try to find the hidden mouse for an additional element of fun.

The Miracle Book

You're holding in your hands a great introduction to the most amazing book in the world: the Bible. Why is the Bible so amazing? Because it's God's book! His servants wrote it, but God made sure it says exactly what He wants. And He kept it safe from its enemies.

God wrote a book because He loves you so much. He wants you to know who He is, what He's like, and what He's done so that you can get to know Him and learn how to live the best life. This book is so unusual that it has to be God's. Here's why.

Amazing Writing: God wrote the book over a period of 1500 years. He used more than 40 people from different countries to write the 66 books of the Bible.

God started by telling a man named Moses how the world began—and how it went wrong. God explained how He formed the nation of Israel and promised that one day He would use Israel to make things right between God and people. God taught Moses about Himself, showed him how life was meant to work, and gave Moses His laws. The Israelites kept Moses' writings safe because they knew they were from God.

After Moses, God chose others, including a priest named Samuel, to write Israel's history. David was a shepherd and later a king. His wonderful praise songs or psalms went in God's book. David's son Solomon wrote God's wisdom for living. Various prophets, people God spoke to, wrote God's messages to His people—and reminded them of God's promise to make things right.

Much later, Jesus, God's Son, fulfilled that promise just as God had said. Jesus' followers wrote His story and what happened after He returned to heaven. Paul and others who loved and followed Jesus with all their hearts wrote down God's instructions, teaching believers the truth and how to live. Finally, John, Jesus' beloved disciple, wrote the final book: God gave him a vision about what would happen at the end when Jesus comes back to Earth.

Amazing Protection: A second thing about the Bible is how much danger it survived. While God's book was being written and after it was finished, God had to keep it safe. You see, God's enemy, Satan, doesn't want anyone to love or follow God. So he keeps trying to stomp out God's Word and destroy the Bible. He kept trying to make people turn away from God and lose or forget about God's ways and laws. But God made sure they were never completely lost or forgotten. One time, Satan got a wicked king to burn some of God's book: God just told the prophet Jeremiah to rewrite that part. About 300 years after Jesus, Satan got the evil emperor Diocletian to arrest and kill God's followers and order that the Bible be destroyed. God kept it safe!

Amazing Copying: In those days there were no printing presses, photocopiers, or computers. The only way to make copies of books was to write them out by hand. God had people copy His book so it would never be completely lost. The copiers were incredibly careful: They counted the words and letters in each book they were copying and compared them. If the numbers didn't match, they destroyed their copy and started again!

God wants everyone to know who He is and how much He loves them. So His next job was to get His book out to everyone. Copying is so slow (imagine copying this book by hand!) that most churches only had one Bible for everyone to share. Then God helped a man named Johann Gutenberg invent an amazing machine called the printing press. It changed the world. The first book he printed was the Bible. Soon many copies were being made—quickly. Satan's plans to destroy God's Book had failed.

Amazing Accuracy: Thanks to God's care, we have His book. But, if it was copied by hand for so long, how can we know it was copied accurately or that we have what was originally written? God took care of that. One way we know this is because of what happened in 1947. An Arab boy searching for his goats near the Dead Sea threw a rock into a cave. Crash! Curious, the boy climbed up and found ancient copies of Bible books that had been hidden in clay pots since the time of Jesus. And guess what? They were almost exactly the same as what we have! The Bible is accurate. In fact, it's the best-kept ancient book there is. We only have a few copies of other

old books, but we have thousands of very old copies of parts of the Bible.

Those who don't believe the Bible say cities and people it names never existed or are wrong. God's not worried. Archaeologists who study old things began digging around for Bible cities. They found them where the Bible said they were. And they keep finding things that confirm that the Bible's true. For example, they've found cities that belonged to the Philistines. They found a sign showing King David really lived. And they found ancient writings that agree with the Bible. God is still working to show that the Bible is accurate and true.

Only God could have created such a book, kept it safe from its enemies, and made sure we can read exactly what He wants. He took all this care because He loves you and wants the best for you.

Questions:

1. What was your favorite part of this story?

2. What did you read that helps you know the Bible is God's book?

Prayer:

Thank God for showing you about Himself and His plan in the Bible and for keeping it safe for you. Ask for help to understand and learn from it.

God Makes a Home

(Genesis 1–2:15)

Our world is so full of wonders that it is very hard to imagine nothing! Close your eyes for a moment. What did you see? Now, close your eyes and put your hands over your ears. What did you see and hear? Now close your eyes, put your hands over your ears, pull both feet off the floor ...well, you get the picture. In the beginning, there was nothing to see, hear, smell, feel, or taste. No food, no toys, no brothers or sisters, no moms or dads. No sun, trees, furry pets, or hugs. Nothing.

Except God.

But God had so much love inside Himself, He

wanted to give some away. He especially wanted children—children who would love Him back. He wanted children who were, in some ways, just like Him. He knew His children would need a special place to live. So God created the earth. For us.

When God said, "Let there be light!" a dazzling bright light appeared out of *nothing*. God enjoyed the light. He divided light from darkness and called the light "day" and the darkness "night." That was the first day.

Then God said, "Let there be a huge space between earth's waters." God called the brilliant blue space "sky." Now some waters were above that space and some below. The second day ended.

God gathered the waters below the sky into crystal seas and piled up dry ground that He called "land." God's excitement grew with His special plan for the land. "Let the land produce plants and trees." And He gave the plants seeds so they could make more plants and trees. Bushes, grass, trees, flowers, and fruit of every kind sprang up. As the third day ended, their perfumes and bright colors dotted the earth.

The next day God filled the sky with lights. He made sparkling stars, gigantic galaxies, and perfect planets out of *nothing*. He made the sun for the day and the moon for the night. These works delighted God. And the fourth day ended.

Then He filled the sea and sky. He made dolphins, sharks, salmon, lobsters, clams, whales, sea urchins, and

stingrays to swim in the waters. He tossed eagles, sparrows, dragonflies, crows, seagulls, mockingbirds, nightingales, and butterflies into the air. As the fifth day ended, all the creatures of the sea and air sang in joy.

At last, God formed every sort of creature that lives on the ground: ants, snails, zebras, snakes, ferrets, impala, flying squirrels, tigers, and everything else. God looked at what He had made and He was so pleased! The special home for His children was ready!

All of God's creatures must have held their breath as He bent over His final creation. He had saved the best until last. As God took some dust from the earth, He shaped it lovingly into a man. He gave him arms and legs to explore the world around him. With eyes and ears, man could see the beauty of colors and shapes and hear the birds sing and the wind sigh. He had a mouth to taste watermelon and a nose to smell roses. God gave man a mind to think and wonder. He gave him a heart to feel and a sense of humor so he could laugh. God also gave the man a spirit and a soul so man could give and receive love—especially the love of God, his Father. Then God blew His breath of life into the man. The man came alive. Imagine waking up and looking into the face of God! Man knew he was special to God and God finally had the child He had longed for.

God named the man Adam. He put him in the Garden of Eden, the most beautiful place in the whole

universe. It exploded with smells, tastes, sounds, colors, and wonders. Adam loved its fascinating creatures, yummy fruit, rushing rivers, and soft breezes.

As God watched him explore this perfect home, He talked with Adam and enjoyed his company. God loved Adam more than anything else He had made. Adam loved God back with all his heart. But one thing was missing: Adam had no wife.

Questions:

1. What are some of the things God made that you really like? Why?

2. Only God can make something out of nothing. But God gave us the ability to create new things from what He has made, such as houses from trees and rings from gold. What things that people make do you really like? Why?

Prayer:

In your prayers tonight, thank God for everything that He made.

The Perfect Companion

(Genesis 2:16–25)

God knew that Adam needed something interesting to do to fill his days. He made Adam that way. So He showed Adam how to take care of all the plants in the Garden of Eden. Then God brought to Adam all the animals, birds, bugs, fish, and reptiles. He told Adam to look at every animal and give it a name. And when Adam named them, it would show that they were in his care.

So Adam began. It was a huge job. God's creatures were amazing and all so different! He saw one bird with huge eyes, pointed ears, and a neck that swiveled almost completely around. The bird blinked and yawned because he usually slept during the day and ate at night. God had woken him up to come see Adam. Adam smiled and named him owl. "Go back to sleep," he said. The owl blinked and flew off to his roost.

Nearby, a large creature with lots of hair around his face, neck, and shoulders lay on his side. He lifted his head to look at Adam. He had sharp teeth, golden-brown fur, and a long tail with a tassel at the end. "You are lion," Adam said. The lion thumped his tail a couple of times, yawned, put his head back down, and dozed.

"What shall I call you?" Adam asked, looking up and up at a tall animal with two horns on her head. Long black lashes ringed her eyes and her jaw moved from side to side as she chewed. Orange-brown patches covered her long graceful neck and strong body. Adam thumped her on the side. "I'll call you. . .Hippo. . .No! Giraffe!"

Adam went from animal to animal to learn what they were like, what they ate, and how God had made them to live. He gave them names just right for them. Names like platypus, orangutan, bear, koala, kangaroo, ant, slug, and horse. Names like eagle, cockatoo, parakeet, peacock, dragonfly, starling, and seagull. Should that black-striped one be skunk or tiger? No, definitely zebra. Tiger was lion's cousin with black stripes. Skunk was the one with a strong smell. Was the one wearing a mask panda or raccoon?

Raccoon! And was that a dolphin, shark, or pussy-willow? No, it was a walrus. The playful one was dolphin.

Adam delighted in naming the creatures God had made. But all the time he kept searching for one who could talk, laugh, or look at the stars with him. There was none. Although Adam loved God more than anything, a part of him was very lonely.

God said, "I'll make a helper who is just right for him. He planned everything in great detail. He wanted someone who matched Adam perfectly and who could be his partner in everything.

So God put Adam into a deep sleep. Then He reached in and took a rib, a part of Adam's inner self, and formed it carefully into a whole new person. This person was like Adam but different. She had her own shape, her own strengths, her own talents, her own likes. She was remarkable! She would be the perfect companion to Adam and could help him look after the world God had given them.

What do you think happened when Adam woke up, rubbed his eyes, and saw this new person God had made? He grinned! He shouted, "Wow!" She was exactly what he had been looking for! "This is bone of my bones and flesh of my flesh. She is like me, my kind of being. She will be called woman because she came out of man."

Adam loved the woman named Eve. He showed her everything in the Garden, shared his favorite fruits with her, and introduced her to all the animals. Adam and Eve could talk about anything as they laughed, played, ate, and worked together in Eden. And they both loved the evenings best, when God came to walk in the Garden with them. They thought their joy would go on forever. That's what God wanted for them. But something was about to happen that would change their lives forever.

Questions:

1. How did God make *you* special?
2. Who are some of the special people God has put in your life? What are some things you like about how God made them?

Prayer:

Thank God for making you special and for giving you the special people you mentioned.

The Serpent and Sin

(Genesis 2:16–17; 3)

Adam and his wife wore no clothes in the Garden but, like newborn babies, they were not ashamed. They were completely comfortable with each other and with God.

As God walked with them He taught them His rules. "You can eat the fruit of any tree that is in the garden," He said. But when they came to the tree of life and the tree of the knowledge of good and evil in the middle of the Garden, God stopped and pointed. "But you mustn't eat the fruit of the tree of the knowledge of good and evil. If you do, you can be sure that you will die." They knew God meant what He said.

Often the man and woman passed by these trees as they worked. They didn't notice the serpent who watched them, waiting for the right time to make his move.

One day, they stopped to inspect the fruit on the tree of the knowledge of good and evil. *I know that God loves me and I can trust what He says,* the woman thought, ready to move on. Suddenly, a beautiful snake slithered out from the tree's branches. She wasn't afraid of him, but knew that serpents were trickier than the other creatures. In fact, this serpent was God's enemy in disguise. Mockingly, he asked, "Did God really say, 'You mustn't eat the fruit of any tree that is in the garden?'"

The woman shook her head. "No," she said. "We can eat the fruit of the trees that are in the garden. But God did say, 'You mustn't eat the fruit of the tree that is in the middle of the garden." She nodded at the tree of the knowledge of good and evil, then added, "God said we mustn't touch it or we'll die."

Now God hadn't said they couldn't touch it. The serpent chuckled as he arched his long neck and wrapped it around a fruit. "Oh, you won't die. God knows that when you eat from this tree, your eyes will be opened. You'll be like God, knowing good and evil."

Stop and think for a moment. It's hard to imagine a world without sin because we've never seen it. Adam and his wife never cried. They were never angry, afraid, or in pain. They were never sick. All the animals obeyed and loved them, curling up beside them at night. Their food

was healthy, tasty, and always ready to eat. Everything they needed was there in the Garden. Absolutely everything. And they could live in peace with God forever.

But, suddenly they wanted more. *Will this fruit really make us wise?* they wondered. Wisdom is good. We'd be like God! So, they decided to listen to the serpent, not God.

Plucking a fruit from the tree, the woman polished and sniffed it. *How could something that looked and smelled so good be bad for me?* she thought. Sinking her teeth into its juicy flesh, she passed it to Adam. He ate too.

What happened next is hard to describe. Like a high-speed train crashing though a brick wall, evil entered their perfect world. And they could never repair the damage they'd done. For the very first time, the man and woman felt fear, confusion, and shame. They were embarrassed and tried to cover their naked bodies with leaves. Their bodies weren't evil, but they thought they were.

And, worst of all, they were afraid of God, their Loving Father. When they heard God coming, they ran away and hid. What would He do to them now?

"Where are you?" God called.

"I heard you in the garden," Adam answered. "I was afraid. I was naked, so I hid."

After a painful silence God asked, "Who told you that you were naked? Have you eaten the fruit of the tree I commanded you not to eat?"

Adam blamed his wife. His wife blamed the serpent.

God was heartbroken. He alone understood the full

price of their disobedience: lives of pain and struggle rather than joy. Instead of living forever, now someday they would have to die. God had lived with them side by side. Now sin separated them from His holiness.

But even now, God had a plan to make things right again in time. God told the serpent, "I'll put hatred between you and the woman. Your children and her children will be enemies. Her son will crush your head. And you'll crush his heel." God meant that one day the woman's descendant, Jesus, would be wounded, but He would destroy God's enemy.

God sent the man and woman out of the Garden of Eden. Angels guarded the entrance so no one could return.

Adam believed the woman would be the mother of all living people and one day her descendant would bring life to the world. So he called her Eve, meaning "living."

Questions:

1. Do you think Adam and Eve made the right choice when they ate the fruit? What should they have done?

2. Name some ways you can obey God and your parents.

Prayer:

Ask God for help to do things His way.

Cain, the Jealous Farmer

(Genesis 4:1–16; Hebrews 11:4; 1 John 3:12)

Adam and Eve began having children. *Perhaps, they thought, our children won't make the same mistakes we did and can get back on track with God.* They would soon learn the sad truth.

Cain, Adam and Eve's first son, stood proudly in his field one day, watching his barley wave in the breeze. Nearby olive trees and vines were bursting with fruit. *What a good farmer I am!* he thought.

"Beautiful day, Cain. God is good!"

Cain looked up to see his younger brother Abel guiding his sheep and goats into their sheepfold. He grunted. "Huh. Fields need more water."

Abel grinned. "Ask God. He'll send what you need."

Cain watched Abel, jealously. "Ask God for this. Trust God for that," he muttered. "Well, maybe an offering wouldn't hurt."

Cain went to his storehouse to find something he could give back to God. *Not that grain,* he thought, passing over the best. *God made me smarter than to waste that.* He dug through his bins and found some old, moldy grain. *Perfect! Can't eat it. Can't plant it. Just right for an offering.* As Cain loaded his grain into a basket, he heard a huge ruckus outside. Abel was sorting through his smelly, noisy animals. "Keep the noise down!" Cain yelled.

Abel smiled. "I'm taking God an offering. He's been so good to me. Just look at this flock! The ewes have healthy babies and the goats have never been stronger!"

"Well, just grab one and shut the rest up," Cain grumped.

Abel couldn't understand Cain. "I can't grab just any lamb, Cain. God deserves the best. Only perfect firstborn males for Him."

Cain shrugged, and went to offer his moldy grain to God. As the smell of Cain's burnt offering rose, he thought smugly, *This should convince God to send rain for my crops.*

Nearby, Abel gave his offering with a full heart. "God, You are so good to me," he said. "I just want to thank You."

God saw the brothers' offerings—and their hearts. He was pleased with Abel and his thankful offering. But He was not pleased with Cain's attitude or his moldy grain. "It's not fair," Cain whined. "God always loved Abel more!"

But God loved Cain just as much and tried to help him. "Why are you angry, Cain? Why are you looking so sad? Do what's right. Then you'll be accepted." Then God warned Cain, "If you don't do what's right, sin is waiting at your door to grab you. It longs to have you. But you must rule over it."

Cain hardly heard God's warning. He kept thinking how unfair life was and how much he hated his brother until one day he invited Abel out into his fields. There Cain's anger exploded! He attacked Abel and killed him. Then he hid the body.

God knew what Cain had done. "Where is your brother Abel?" He asked. If Cain confessed and asked God to forgive him, perhaps God could still work with Cain to change his heart. All heaven waited hopefully for Cain's answer.

But Cain lied, "I don't know. Am I supposed to look after my brother?"

"Oh, Cain," God cried. "What have you done? Listen! Your brother's blood is crying out to Me from the ground." God looked at Cain sadly. "I'm putting a curse on you," He said. "I'm driving you away from the ground. . .It won't produce its crops for you anymore. You'll be a restless person who wanders around on the earth."

"You're punishing me more than I can take!" Cain complained. "Today you are driving me away from the land. I'll be hidden from You. . . . Anyone who finds me wil kill me."

God shook His head, "No. Anyone who kills you will be paid back seven times." The LORD put a mark on Cain so anyone who found him wouldn't kill him.

So Cain went away from the LORD and went to live in the land of Nod. Adam and Eve lost two sons to sin. And sin would continue to grow in the hearts of their grandchildren, great grandchildren, great, great grandchildren, and even until today. Sin is passed down. It wants to grab every person.

Question:

God did not send Cain away. Cain left God. What does this tell you about God's love—even for a murderer?

What can you do to make things right with God when you sin?

Prayer:

Ask God for help to speak and act kindly to others. Mention anyone you're having trouble getting along with.

Crazy or Right?

(Genesis 6:1–9:17; 11:10)

Boom! Shem felt the whole ark shake as God closed the giant door. How he wished his friends and neighbors had listened. Now it was too late. Noah's family had been inside the ark for seven days and Shem had wondered if the flood would really happen. But as the door slammed, he knew. Seth thought about the many years getting ready for this moment.

At times, Shem thought his dad was crazy! Why would anyone build a huge boat in their backyard without any way to get it to water?

"God told me to, Shem," Noah had said, "and that's enough for me."

All his life, Noah did what God said was right. And God noticed. God promised Noah if he followed His instructions, his family would be saved.

But saved from what? Shem had wondered. *What does Dad know that no one else seems to?* God had spoken to Noah's heart. The world was full of wickedness. People stole, beat each other up, lied, cheated, and killed. This caused God so much pain that He was sorry He had made man. He was sending a great flood to wash the world clean again. But God would save Noah, his wife and three sons—Shem, Ham and Japheth—and their three wives. Not to mention the animals. God said they must take two of each kind. That's why the ark had to be so huge. And what a boat it was! It had taken most of Shem's life to build it—and he was almost ninety-seven!

Shem and his brothers had chopped down and hauled trees, squared them, and tied them in place with reed ropes. It was backbreaking work. Their wives had boiled pitch for waterproofing and gathered supplies. All the while the people mocked: "Hey Shem, gonna build a lake too? Boy are you dumb!"

Shem's heart ached for his friends. He tried to convince them to stop sinning and perhaps God would save them, too. But they only laughed at him. "Yeah, right! Whatever you say, Shem."

Finally, Shem and his brothers lashed the final reeds onto the roof so no water could ever get through. The ark

was ready. Then Noah and his family went into the ark to wait for rain.

Perhaps people will finally believe us, Shem thought, as the family watched a parade of animals come to the ark. They laughed in wonder and pointed to each new animal they'd never seen before. Monkeys and apes swung aboard. Hippo, elephant, and bear couples lumbered up the ramp. Cheetahs, lions, and pussycats sauntered in. Dogs, wolves, aardvarks, cows, sheep, mice, lizards, doves, parrots. . .you name them, they walked, slithered, jumped, or flew inside.

Now the door was closed. No one else could enter. Shem looked sadly one last time at the people outside the boat as it began to rain. And rain and rain! It pounded on the ark's roof and flooded the fields in minutes. Soon the ark began to float. It rained for what seemed forever. Then sudden silence fell on the fortieth day. Shem looked out the window of the ark. He saw nothing but water. *Nothing!*

For about a year, they worked hard to feed and clean up after all the animals on board. *I'm sick of being on this boat*, Shem thought. *But where else could we go?* Besides, God watched over them. Finally, the land dried enough for them to leave. Shem and his wife stepped outside, gulping in the fresh, clean air. The animals kicked up their heels as they scampered down the ramp, delighted to be on solid ground again!

Noah thanked and worshipped God right away. This

pleased God. He said, "I'm making a promise to you, Noah, to your children and the whole earth." Suddenly a band of sparkling colors arched across the sunny sky. "The rainbow will be the sign of My promise: waters will never again destroy all life."

As Shem looked at the new world around him, he knew he'd never forget sin's awful power. *God's given our family a fresh start, he thought. I promise to do my best to follow Him and teach my children to do the same.*

Questions:

1. How might you feel if God told you to do something like Noah that would make your friends laugh at you? Would it be hard? Why or why not?

2. When other kids are doing wrong, how can you do right?

Prayer:

Ask God's help to do things His way—even when others aren't.

The Promise of Laughter

(Genesis 12:1–5; 13:5–12; 15:1–7;
17:1–7, 15–21; 18:1–15; 21:1–7)

In time, the world had many people again. But few of them were looking for God. Abram, one of Shem's descendants, was different. He wanted to know God and obey Him completely. Abram learned that when he talked to God, God spoke back to him deep in his heart.

One day Abram pushed back the colorful cloth door of his home. He smiled at his wife Sarai as he entered. He had some big news.

"God just spoke to me," Abram said. "He wants us to leave this place."

Abram often talked with God. Sarai was used to Abram telling her things that God said. But this was a big decision. It meant leaving their home and family behind. "Where would we go?" Sarai asked. "And for how long?"

"God said He would show us where to go. I don't think we'll ever come back." Abram took his wife's hands. "Sarai, God also said He will bless me and He'll make me into a great nation! That must mean He will give us children!"

Sarai's eyes filled with tears. How they wanted a child! She and Abram were already old. If they had a baby now, it would be a miracle. Pausing only for a moment, Sarai decided to trust Abram—and God.

"Let's go, then," she said.

Abram took Sarai, servants, sheep, goats, donkeys, and camels and followed God. They looked like a brown cloud moving across the rough, dry land as the animals churned up dust with their feet. You can imagine how delighted they were to reach Canaan after months traveling at the animals' pace and eating dust for lunch! Abram looked at the rolling green hills, lush pasture, and stately trees. He knew in his heart this was the place God promised to him and his descendants.

God blessed Abram. The baaing, bleating, and hee-hawing of his growing flocks constantly reminded him of God's kindness! But Abram still had no children. One day, Abram reminded God about His promise. "Oh, LORD," he cried, "You haven't given me any children. So a servant in my house will get everything I own."

God heard Abram's sorrow. He answered, "A son will come from your own body. He will get everything you own." God showed Abram all the stars in the inky black sky. "That's how many children you'll have." *Wow!* Abram thought. *God has big plans. That's even more than I can count!*

But Sarai was struggling. It had been eleven years since they left home. Maybe God wanted something different than they thought. She told Abram, "Take another wife. Maybe she'll give you a son." So Abram did. And Ishmael was born. *At last,* Abram thought, *This is the heir God promised.*

Abram was wrong. When Ishmael was 13 and Abram was 99, God repeated His promise. "Your name will be Abraham [meaning father of many]," He said. "As for Sarai your wife. . .Her name will be Sarah [meaning princess]. I will give her My blessing. You can be sure that I will give you a son by her."

Sarah? Abraham laughed to himself, *At her age?* But God was serious. "By this time next year Sarah will have a son by you. And you will name him Isaac [meaning laughter]. . .I'll make him into a great nation."

What should I do? Abraham thought. *I don't want to disappoint Sarah again.* It was hard to keep hoping after twenty years. *I won't tell her this time,* he decided. So God made sure Sarah heard the news for herself.

Not long afterward, three strangers came to Abraham's camp. (Abraham didn't know they were

messengers from God.) After dinner they asked, "Where's your wife, Sarah?"

"She's in the tent," he answered, pointing.

Then one of them said, "I'll return to you about this time next year. Your wife Sarah will have a son."

Sarah heard. *Impossible*, she laughed to herself. "After I'm worn out and Abraham's old, will I really know the joy of having a baby?"

"Why did Sarah laugh?" the messenger asked. "Is anything too hard for the LORD?"

Well, nothing is too hard for the LORD. Sarah soon became pregnant—at 90—and gave birth to a baby boy! Abraham and Sarah had laughed at God's message, now they laughed *with* God in joy. They named the baby Isaac, "laughter."

Questions:

1. Why did Sarah laugh at the idea of having a baby when she was 90 years old?
2. God always keeps His promises. Do you know some things God promises *you* in the Bible?

Prayer:

Talk to God about His promises in the Bible. Then thank God that He can do all things.

Where's the Lamb?

(Genesis 22:1–19)

Isaac grew up knowing he was a miracle baby and that God had big plans for his life!

One night his father said, "Sleep well. Tomorrow we go to Moriah to sacrifice to God." (This meant they would thank God for His goodness by offering Him an animal and burning it on an altar.)

"Just you and me?" Isaac asked, eagerly. Abraham nodded.

As the sun painted the sky pink, Isaac bounced out of bed, dressed quickly, and went to help Abraham saddle the donkey. Two servants strapped on supplies and put wood for the fire on top. Then they set out.

Isaac loved having time alone with his dad. Abraham answered his endless questions, laughed at his jokes, and paused to let him climb the giant rocks and explore the caves they passed. Abraham watched him as if he didn't want to miss a thing. Isaac could feel his dad's love. He knew he could trust his dad no matter what!

Their day was filled with sunshine, babbling brooks, green pastures, hardy trees, lush orchards, and strong mountains. What a beautiful land they lived in! God said He would give this land to Abraham and his descendants. *I'm a descendant*, thought Isaac. *That must include me!*

When they reached Moriah, Abraham told the servants, "Stay here with the donkey. The boy and I will go over there and worship," he nodded to the mountain. "We'll come back."

Isaac carried the wood while Abraham carried the knife and coals for the fire. Isaac was very excited. He knew that God often spoke to Abraham as he worshipped. Isaac hoped that he would hear God, too. As they scrambled up the rocky slope, Abraham became very quiet. He seemed to be thinking about something that made him very sad. So Isaac was quiet, too, as they built an altar out of rocks and placed the wood on top for the fire the way they always did. But something was different here.

Finally, Isaac said, "Dad? The fire and wood are here.

But where's the lamb for the sacrifice?"

Abraham took a deep breath and let it out. "God Himself will provide the lamb for the burnt offering, my son." Suddenly his dad stood in front of Isaac with a rope. "Give me your hands," he said. Isaac held out his hands and Abraham tied them. Then he tied Isaac's feet and lifted him on top of the wood. Isaac swallowed hard and looked into his father's face.

"Dad?" he whispered. Isaac was so afraid, nothing else came out of his mouth.

Tears streamed down Abraham's face. "God told me to offer you as a sacrifice, Isaac. I must obey."

Isaac gulped. Even now he knew his father loved him and didn't want to hurt him. "Yes, father," he croaked. "But didn't God promise to make a great nation through me and my descendants?"

"Yes, He did," Abraham nodded. "But I know I still must obey, even if I don't understand."

Isaac closed his eyes and held his breath as Abraham lifted the knife.

Instantly a voice boomed, "Abraham! Don't lay a hand on the boy!" Abraham crumpled before the altar and then pulled Isaac into his arms. They knew God was speaking. Abraham untied his son and they hugged each other for a long time, crying in relief and loving one another more than they ever had before.

"Now I know that you have respect for God. You have not held back from Me your son, your only son,"

God said. Abraham had passed God's test. God looked for a man who would be completely obedient to Him so He could begin to build a people that would follow Him. Abraham proved to God that he was that man.

Suddenly something thrashed in a nearby bush. "Baa!" A ram was caught by his horns! So Abraham sacrificed the ram to God. He called that place, "The LORD Will Provide."

God spoke again: "I will certainly bless you. I will make your children after you as many as the stars in the sky. . . . All nations on earth will be blessed because of your children. All of that will happen because you have obeyed Me."

As Abraham and Isaac returned home, Isaac knew, no matter how much he trusted his father, he could trust God more. God had a plan for him. As long as Isaac followed Him, God would make sure it came true.

Questions:

1. Obeying God can be hard sometimes. How did Abraham learn to trust God?
2. What are some things you find hard to obey? Why?

Prayer:

Talk to God about the times you've found it hard to obey. Ask Him for the ability to do what pleases Him.

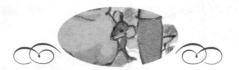

Grabbing the Promise

(Genesis 25:19–34; 27:1–28:9; Hebrews 12:16–17)

Isaac paced the ground outside the tent where his wife Rebekah was giving birth. Suddenly he heard a baby cry. Then a second baby cried. Twins! Isaac rushed to see them and give them names. The firstborn twin was all red and hairy. They named him Esau (meaning "hairy"). Amazingly, the second twin came out holding the heel of his brother! They called him Jacob (meaning "he grabs the heel," or "he cheats").

Jacob was born only minutes after Esau, but *second*. In those days, that was important because the oldest son got his father's blessing and inherited twice as much as his brothers. God's promises passed down to him too, all because he was born first.

"It'll be different with you, Jacob," his mother told him as he grew older. "When I was pregnant, God told me that the older, Esau, would serve the younger—you!" Jacob already knew the story, but how could that happen? His father seemed to love Esau most. Esau was a hunter, and Isaac loved the wild meat he brought. Jacob was quiet and preferred to stay at home. So Jacob began to plot a way to steal the family's greatest treasure: the promise of God's friendship given first to Abraham and then to Isaac.

One day Esau came home hungry. Food! He had to have some! He found Jacob stirring a pot of lentil stew. "Quick! Give me some," he said. "I'm starving."

Jacob thought, *Now's my chance!* "First promise me your firstborn rights," he demanded.

Esau shrugged. "Okay. All my rights as the oldest son are yours." It was that easy. Esau seemed to care little about his special place in the family, or God's promises. He only wanted to eat.

When Isaac became very old and blind, he called Esau to his bedside. "Esau," he said, "I don't know how much longer I'll live. Go hunting and cook some meat the way I like it. When you bring it, I'll give you my blessing."

Rebekah heard what Isaac said to Esau and rushed to tell Jacob. Jacob's heart thumped. Would Esau get the firstborn blessing after all? But Rebekah had a plan to "help" God give it to Jacob. She forgot that God never

wants us to lie, even if we think we have a good reason. "Get me two young goats. I'll cook them the way your father likes. When you bring them, he'll think you're Esau and give you his blessing."

Rebekah covered Jacob's arms and neck with goat skins and dressed him in Esau's best clothes. Now, thought Rebekah, *Isaac will never guess it's Jacob.*

"Here, father," Jacob said, bringing a tray of food to Isaac.

"Who is it?" Isaac asked.

"Esau," Jacob lied. "I brought you some wild meat."

But Isaac was suspicious. "Come near so I can touch you," he said. He felt the hairy goatskins and smelled Esau's clothes. "It's the voice of Jacob but the smell and hands of Esau." Again Isaac asked, "Are you really my son Esau?"

"I am," Jacob repeated. So Isaac ate Rebekah's meat. Then he gave Jacob the firstborn blessing: God's promise to build a great nation through him and his children. And his brother would serve him.

Jacob left his father's tent quickly. He knew there would be trouble when Esau found out what he had done.

Sure enough. Esau returned from hunting and took his meat to Isaac. Jacob and Rebecca heard Isaac roar: "Jacob stole your blessing!"

"Bless me too, father," Esau begged.

Isaac could not take back Esau's blessing from Jacob, so he gave Esau the blessing he had planned for Jacob: "You'll live far from the richness of the earth and you'll

serve your brother. But you'll grow restless and throw off the heavy load he'll put on you."

Esau was so angry that he wanted to kill Jacob. Rebekah worried for Jacob's safety. So she convinced Isaac to send Jacob to her brother in Paddan Aram to find a wife.

Isaac called Jacob to his tent and said, "Go and take a wife from our relatives in Paddan Aram. May the mighty God bless you. May He give you children. . . . May He give you and your children after you the blessing He gave Abraham. Then you can take over the land where you now live as an outsider."

So Rebekah's plan worked: Jacob escaped from Esau. But Rebekah would never see Jacob again.

Questions:

1. Sometimes we think that doing wrong things will get us ahead. It doesn't. What did Jacob lose when he cheated his brother?
2. Have you ever told a lie thinking it would help? What happened?

Prayer:

Ask God to help you to be truthful and to trust Him.

The Cheater Is Cheated

(Genesis 28:10–33:20)

Jacob was tired! He lay on the hard ground, using a rock for a pillow. Esau must hate me, he thought, tossing and turning. *I should never have stolen his blessing! Will I ever see home again?* Finally, he fell asleep.

God saw Jacob's fear and gave him a message as he slept. In Jacob's dreams, angels went up and down a stairway to heaven with God at the top. "I am the God of your grandfather Abraham and the God of Isaac," He said. "I will give you and your children after you the land on which you're lying. All nations on earth will be blessed because of you and your children after you. I am with you. I'll watch over you everywhere you go. And I'll bring you back to this land."

Jacob woke up encouraged. "May God be with me," he said. "May He watch over me on this journey. . . . Then you, LORD, will be my God. . . . and I'll give you a tenth of everything you give me."

When Jacob reached the well outside Paddan Aram, he met a beautiful girl named Rachel watering her sheep. "I'll work for you for seven years to get your younger daughter Rachel for my wife," Jacob told his uncle Laban, Rachel's father. It was a deal.

Seven years flew by for Jacob. Then came his wedding day! But the next morning he found he had married Leah, Rachel's older sister. Laban had tricked him! Now Jacob knew how it felt to be the one who was cheated.

"The younger can't marry before the older," Laban explained. "Now I'll give you Rachel too—for another seven years' work." (In those days, God allowed men more than one wife.)

God's blessing on Jacob also helped Laban. Laban's flocks increased and he became a rich man. Laban didn't want Jacob to leave, but he didn't want to pay Jacob for his work, either. So Laban found other ways to cheat Jacob.

Jacob said, "I'll keep working for you if you give me only the dark lambs and spotted or speckled goats." Laban agreed, but hid the dark and spotted animals in his flocks from Jacob. Then God blessed Jacob with many newborn spotted and speckled goats and dark lambs. Laban kept changing the rules, but God always blessed Jacob.

Jacob prospered so much that Laban's sons became jealous. "He's taking our inheritance," they complained.

Jacob's family grew too, until he had eleven sons and one daughter: Reuben, Simeon, Levi, Judah, Dan, Naphtali, Gad, Asher, Issachar, Zebulun, Joseph, and Dinah.

Finally, God spoke to Jacob. "Go back to your father's land and to your relatives," He said. "I'll be with you."

So Jacob left with his family and the herds God had given him. As Jacob began to recognize the hills and valleys of his home, he wondered, *Does Esau still hate me?* He sent a messenger, saying, "I've been with our uncle Laban. I have cattle, donkeys, sheep, goats, and servants. Please think kindly of me."

The messenger returned, saying, "Esau is coming to meet you—with 400 men."

Jacob shuddered and prayed for protection. "God, You told me to go home," he said. "You've blessed me even though I didn't deserve it. Please save my family." Then he sent servants with animals as gifts for Esau, hoping to win his forgiveness.

That night, Jacob didn't sleep. A mysterious man appeared and wrestled with Jacob until morning. When the sky began to lighten, Jacob was determined to win. He said, "I won't let you go until you bless me."

"What's your name?" the man asked.

"Jacob," he answered. Suddenly Jacob remembered his name meant "cheater" and recalled all the times he'd cheated others. Jacob was ashamed.

"Your name will not be Jacob anymore. Instead, it will be Israel," the man said. Israel means "he wrestles with God." Then he left and Jacob realized the man had

been a messenger from God!

Jacob looked up. There was Esau with 400 men! Jacob bowed down, showing Esau he respected him and was sorry. Suddenly Esau ran toward Jacob. He threw his arms around his neck and kissed him. They cried together. Then Esau asked, "Who are these people?"

"They're the children God has so kindly given to me. And the animals are a gift for you."

Esau laughed, "I have plenty. I don't need them." But Jacob insisted.

God forgave Jacob and Jacob was a changed man. God brought Jacob and his family home just as He had promised and blessed Rachel with another son, Benjamin. So Jacob, also called Israel, had twelve sons to begin a great nation.

Questions:

1. Forgiveness is right, even when it's hard. Do you think Esau forgave Jacob because of Jacob's gifts or because it was the right thing to do? Why?
2. Is there anyone you need to forgive right now? Who?

Prayer:

Thank God for forgiving you when you make mistakes. Ask Him for help to forgive others.

Dad's Favorite Becomes a Slave!

(Genesis 37:1–36; 39:1–23; 42:21)

Joseph's brothers glared at him, "Tattle tale!" they said. They hated him because he was their father's favorite—and his telling tales didn't help. Joseph squirmed. Then he heard his father call. *Just in time*, Joseph thought, running to his father's tent.

Jacob held up a colorful coat embroidered in gold. "Try it on," he urged. It was worth a fortune and fit Joseph perfectly! *This proves that father loves me best*, Joseph gloated. His brothers wore plain work clothes. Hugging his father, Joseph ran to show off to his brothers. But they *weren't* pleased. They were jealous! They couldn't say even one kind word to Joseph.

One morning Joseph woke up and rushed to where his brothers were eating breakfast. "Listen," he said. "I dreamed that we were working in the fields and your bundles of grain bowed down to mine."

"Do you plan to be king over us?" they asked, hating him even more.

Not long afterward, Joseph's brothers were away with the flocks. Jacob said to Joseph, "Go to your brothers. See how they are doing. Also, see how the flocks are doing. Then come back and tell me."

Joseph put on his special coat and set off. When he found his brothers, he grinned. But they grabbed him roughly and tore his coat off. "Come. Let's kill him," they said. "Let's say that a wild animal ate him up. Then we'll see whether his dreams will come true."

Reuben disagreed, "Let's not spill any blood. Throw him into this empty well here in the desert." He winked at Joseph, planning to return later and rescue him. So Joseph's brothers threw him in the well and calmly ate their lunch.

Joseph was scared. "Please! Let me out!" he cried. But his brothers ignored him. *Surely it's a joke!* he thought. It was cold in the well and he missed his coat.

Finally the brothers lifted Joseph out of the well. When Joseph saw the hatred on their faces, he looked frantically for Reuben. Reuben was gone and Judah was bargaining with some traders—over *him!* Joseph couldn't believe it. Judah held up a heavy bag of coins. "Well,

Joseph, you're finally worth something," he taunted. "This way we're rid of you forever—and we get paid for it!"

"Don't do this!" Joseph begged. But they ignored his tears. A trader dragged Joseph to the line of camels and tied him among other slaves. As the camels started off, Joseph looked back. His brothers were counting their money. They didn't even watch him leave.

Reuben returned later and found Joseph missing. He was so upset that he tore his clothes. "Now what'll I do?" he wailed. So they killed a goat, smeared its blood on Joseph's coat, and took it to Jacob. "It's my son's robe! A wild animal has eaten him up!" Jacob cried. He never got over Joseph's loss.

Meanwhile the traders took Joseph to the slave markets in Egypt where he was prodded, poked, and pinched. Joseph was seventeen, healthy, and strong. The slave traders expected to get a good price for him. Joseph was so hurt by his brothers' betrayal that he didn't care what happened to him when Potiphar, captain of the Egyptian palace guard, bought him as a slave.

Joseph worked hard and did his best for his new master. God blessed Joseph. Everything he did succeeded. Potiphar noticed. He kept promoting Joseph until Joseph was in charge of everything Potiphar owned. He said, "With you in charge, Joseph, I don't worry about anything!"

Now Joseph was a handsome man. Potiphar's wife noticed. She wanted to secretly have him love her like a husband. Joseph refused. Day after day she begged him. "I

can't!" Joseph said. "Potiphar trusts me. How could I do such an evil thing? How could I sin against God?"

One day when Joseph was in the house alone with her, Potiphar's wife grabbed him. But Joseph ran as fast as he could, even leaving his coat in her hand. She was furious. When Potiphar came home she lied, saying, "Your slave attacked me. When I screamed for help, he ran away and forgot his coat."

Angry and disappointed, Potiphar arrested Joseph and put him in prison with the king's prisoners. Joseph had done nothing wrong. But he thought, *I'm in God's hands. I'll trust and serve Him wherever I am.* So Joseph kept working hard and doing what was right. Soon, the prison warden put him in charge. With Joseph in charge, the warden didn't worry about anything. And God blessed everything Joseph did.

Questions:

1. Think of a time you felt you were treated unfairly. What happened? How did you react?
2. How can you be more like Joseph, especially when things seem unfair?

Prayer:

Thank God for taking care of you no matter what happens. Ask for help to always trust Him.

Ex-Prisoner Rules Egypt!

(Genesis 40–47)

Prison is not a good place to be! But Joseph was learning that if he obeyed and trusted God, God blessed him—even in prison. One day, Joseph noticed that two important prisoners, Pharaoh's baker and wine taster, were unhappy.

"We had dreams," they said. "But nobody can explain them."

"God can," Joseph said. He told them what the dreams meant. Within three days they came true! When the wine taster returned to the palace, Joseph said, "Remember me." But for two years, he forgot about Joseph.

Joseph now was 30 years old. *It's been so long,* he

thought. *Will the dreams God gave me still come true?*

Soon a guard came for Joseph. "Wash up," he said. "Pharaoh's had a dream and wants to see you." *At last,* Joseph thought, *the wine taster remembered!*

"I hear you can explain dreams." Pharaoh leaned back in his gold throne, studying Joseph.

"I can't do it," Joseph replied. "But God will give Pharaoh the answer he wants."

"In one dream," Pharaoh began, "I was standing by the Nile River. Seven fat, healthy cows came up out of the water. Then seven ugly and skinny cows came and gobbled up the fat cows but stayed so skinny no one could tell they'd eaten. I also dreamed of seven full, good heads of grain. Then seven weak, shriveled heads of grain swallowed them up."

Joseph answered, "God showed you what's about to happen. Both your dreams mean the same thing. The seven fat cows and healthy heads of grain mean seven good years. The seven skinny cows and shriveled heads of grain mean seven bad years. We'll have seven years with plenty of food. But then we'll have seven years of famine. Two dreams mean it will happen for sure."

"Put someone wise in charge," Joseph suggested. "Have him store some of the harvest during the good years. Then people will have food to eat during the famine."

Pharaoh said, "Since God showed you this, Joseph, I'm putting you in charge." He put the signet ring, used to seal royal orders, on Joseph's finger. He gave him fine

linen robes and placed a gold chain around Joseph's neck. Joseph rode in a chariot, and all the people honored him.

For seven years, Egypt had lots of food. Joseph stored up grain. When the good years ended, people everywhere were desperate for food. But in Egypt, they had plenty.

Far away in Canaan, Jacob's family grew hungry. Jacob told his sons, "Go to Egypt and buy some grain, or we'll starve."

Joseph's brothers went to Egypt and bowed down to Joseph like everyone else, asking for grain. The brothers didn't recognize Joseph. But Joseph knew them right away. *So!* he thought, *my dreams came true exactly as God showed me. But have my brothers changed?* he wondered. He decided to test them.

"You're spies!" he said. "You've come to see the places where our land isn't guarded very well!" Then he arrested them.

Reuben said to his brothers, "God's punishing us. Joseph begged for help but we refused." Joseph kept Simeon as a hostage and told the others to go home and bring back their youngest brother, Benjamin. Joseph had one more test for them.

When they came back, Joseph had his servant hide a precious cup in Benjamin's grain. Then he pretended to arrest Benjamin for stealing it! Judah cried, "How can I go back to my father if the boy isn't with me? Don't let me see the pain and suffering that would come to my father."

He begged Joseph to punish him instead of Benjamin. (Benjamin was Jacob's favorite after Joseph disappeared.)

Hearing that, Joseph *knew* his brothers had changed. They cared for each other and were sorry for what they'd done. "I'm Joseph your brother", he said. "Don't blame yourselves anymore for selling me as a slave. God made me ruler of Egypt so that I could save many people. Go get father and the family. I'll take care of you."

Joseph's brothers ran to him and hugged him. Everyone talked at once, crying tears of joy and relief. Then they hurried home to tell Jacob. He could hardly believe it! But God said to him, "Go. I'll make you a nation and one day bring you back here."

For all those difficult years Joseph did things God's way. And God kept His promises.

Questions:

1. How do you think Joseph felt when his brothers kneeled in front of him and he remembered his dreams?
2. Joseph trusted God to work things out. What should you do when things go wrong?

Prayer:

Ask God's help to trust Him to work things out for you as He did for Joseph.

Brother in a Basket

(Exodus 1:1–2:10)

Miriam scrambled over stones and ducked behind a pile of straw. "*Crack!*" A slave driver snapped his whip. Miriam hoped it wasn't at her dad, Amram. He always came home sore and exhausted from making bricks out of clay and straw—sometimes with whip marks.

After Joseph had died, a new Pharaoh took over and made the Israelites his slaves. Now Pharaoh ordered the women to keep only baby girls. But Shiphrah and Puah had kept many baby boys alive, including Miriam's brother Aaron. Her mother was having another baby. She had to find them! *I hope it's a girl!* she thought as she raced to the village. "Where are Shiphrah and Puah?" she shouted.

"Try the square," someone answered.

Miriam ran to the square. Puah was resting by the well. "Puah, come quickly," she called. "Mother's having the baby." They quickly wove their way through the mud shacks, past the work crews, to Miriam's home.

Miriam watched three-year-old Aaron while Puah helped her mom. Finally, Miriam heard a tiny cry. Puah's eyes were sad. "It's a boy," she said. "But he's a strong one. Perhaps God will be merciful and he'll be safe." Miriam tried to smile.

For three months, the family kept the baby quiet. But as he grew, his cries grew too. One night Miriam's mother nodded at the baby. "He's getting too big to hide, Miriam. Pharaoh says we must throw boys into the river. We can't hide him forever. We'll put him in a basket and trust God to protect him!"

When the basket was done, Miriam helped her mother cover it with sticky tar, making it waterproof. Early the next morning, they wrapped the baby in a tiny blanket, laid him in the basket, and carried him to the river. The basket would be hard to see nestled among the thick reeds. Hopefully the crocodiles wouldn't see it. "Keep watch over him and see what happens," Miriam's mother said.

Sitting in the shade of some palm trees, Miriam enjoyed the gentle whisper of wind through the

leaves. She was almost dozing when she heard voices!
She peeked out and saw well-dressed Egyptian women
coming. The one in the middle must be a princess:
Miriam had never seen anyone so beautiful! The
princess and her servants cooled themselves in the
river. Suddenly the baby started crying. *Now what?*
Miriam grew nervous. LORD, *please keep my baby
brother safe!*

The princess lifted her head. She'd heard! She said
something and one of the women found the basket and
carried it to her. Miriam crept close to hear. These
women knew the law. Her brother was in danger!

When they removed the basket lid, the baby stopped
crying and gurgled happily. The princess smiled and
played with him. "This is one of the Hebrew babies," she
said. She looked toward the palace, then cradled the baby
against her shoulder. *Maybe she would keep him,* Miriam
thought. She stood up. "Excuse me," she said, her voice
shaky and small.

Guards sprang toward her. The princess held up her
hand. "Wait. What is it?"

"Do you want me to go and get one of the
Hebrew women?" Miriam asked. "She could nurse the
baby for you."

The princess smiled and nodded, "Yes. Go." Miriam
raced off to tell her mother what had happened.
Jochebed came and bowed to the princess. "Take this
baby," the princess said. "Nurse him for me. I'll pay you.

We'll call him 'Moses.'"

Grinning, Miriam and her mother took baby Moses home. As he grew, Miriam helped her parents tell Moses all about their people and about God so he would always know who he was.

When Moses was old enough to leave, his mother and Miriam took him to the palace where he grew up as a prince.

Questions:

1. Why was Miriam afraid when the Egyptian princess found Moses?
2. God saved baby Moses. Do you have a story of a time when God looked after you? (Parents tell a story you have.)

Prayer:

Thank God for being your Father and looking after you. Ask Him to protect you like baby Moses.

The Burning Bush Miracle

(Exodus 2:11–4:31)

The blazing sun beat down on the rocks below Mount Sinai. Moses sipped water from a goatskin container and tossed a rock to make a goat back away from the cliff. As a shepherd, he had lots of time to think. *I'm sure a long way from the palace and Egypt, he sighed. I thought God had something for me to do there, but no more. Not after what I did!*

Moses remembered the smell of sweat and the slave's cries on that fateful day. A slave—an Israelite—had fallen under a load of bricks. The Egyptian slave driver whipped the man, yelling, "Get up!"

"Stop!" Moses shouted. Even though Moses lived in

Pharaoh's palace, the Israelites were his people. It angered him to see them so mistreated. Moses, a strong young man, knocked the slave driver to the ground and killed him. Looking around to see if any Egyptian had seen what he'd done, Moses buried the man in the sand. If Pharaoh found out, he would have Moses killed.

Sure enough, Pharaoh heard. So Moses ran for his life to Midian—forty years ago now. *I did a terrible thing that day,* Moses shuddered. *But God was merciful and gave me a new life here.* He smiled remembering the day he met Zipporah, now his wife, and her kind father Jethro. *And I know this desert and the mountains like the back of my hand.*

Suddenly, a bright light yanked Moses from his daydreams. A bush near a large rock spouted golden flames. Fire in the desert could mean real trouble!

Moses checked the goats, then stared again at the strange fire. He frowned. *That bush should be ashes by now and the fire should be spreading,* he thought.

Suddenly a voice from the bush said: "Moses! Do not come any closer. Take off your sandals. The place you are standing on is holy ground." Moses jumped! *What's going on here?* he wondered, quickly untying his sandals.

"I am the God of your father. I am the God of Abraham." God spoke from the bush. "I've seen My people suffer in Egypt. . . . I've come down to save them. I'll bring them into a good land. It has a lot of room. It is a land that has plenty of milk and honey. . . . So now, go.

I'm sending you to Pharaoh. I want you to bring the Israelites out of Egypt."

God had Moses' complete attention now! "Me? Who am I?" Moses could think of a hundred reasons why he was *not* the right one. After all, he was 80 years old. And what about that Egyptian he'd killed?

"I'll be with you," God answered. He told Moses that the elders would listen, but Pharaoh wouldn't let the people go until He had sent many miracles to convince him.

Then the LORD told Moses to throw down his wooden shepherd's staff. The staff began to slither. It was a snake! Moses shuddered when God told him to pick it up again. He *hated* snakes. Carefully inching toward the snake as it crawled away, he lunged to grab it by the tail. In his hand, it was wood again! This sign would prove God had sent Moses to the elders.

And can you believe it? Moses *still* argued with God? "LORD," he said, "I've never been a good speaker."

"Who makes man able to talk?" God asked. "Who makes him unable to hear or speak? It is I, the LORD. Now go. I will help you speak. I'll teach you what to say."

Moses begged one last time, "LORD, please send someone else to do it."

God knew Moses was the right man. In fact, He'd chosen Moses for this job before Moses was even born. Still God knew Moses was scared. "What about your brother Aaron? He can speak well. He's already on his

way to meet you. . . . Speak to him. Put your words in his mouth. Tell him what to say. I will help both of you speak. . . . But take this wooden staff in your hand. You will be able to do miraculous signs with it."

Moses picked up the wooden staff that God would use in a mighty way. He returned the flocks to Jethro and told him what had happened. Then he set off with his family. Along the way, just as God said, they met Aaron. They were so happy to see one another! It had been so long! They laughed, cried, and told their stories all the way back to Egypt.

The brothers met with the elders as God had told them. The Israelites believed when they heard that God cared, bowing down to worship Him. Now the only thing left to do was convince Pharaoh.

Questions:

1. Which miracle in this story do you like best? Why?
2. If God spoke from a burning bush telling you to do something, what would you say?

Prayer:

Ask God to go with you wherever you go, just like Moses.

Stubbornness and Plagues

(Exodus 5–10)

Moses climbed the familiar palace steps with his brother Aaron. Memories flooded his mind as they crossed the huge, granite hallway, and approached the throne. There was a new Pharaoh since Moses had left Egypt. *Maybe he will listen and believe what we say*, Moses hoped.

"The LORD is the God of Israel," Aaron told Pharaoh. "He says, 'Let My people go. Then they'll be able to hold a feast in My honor in the desert.'"

Pharaoh frowned. Egypt had many gods. In fact, some people thought Pharaoh himself was a god. "No!" he said. "Who is this God? Why should I obey Him?"

That same day, after Moses and Aaron left, Pharaoh called his officials. "The Israelites must not have enough to do or they wouldn't ask me to go to the desert," he said. "Tell them they must make the same number of bricks but now find their own straw."

The Egyptians made the slaves work even harder. Now they were angry with Moses.

Moses was puzzled. He prayed, "LORD, why did you send me? Look what's happened! The people are worse off than ever."

God answered, "Now you'll see what I will do to Pharaoh. Because of My powerful hand, he will let the people of Israel go."

Moses and Aaron returned to Pharaoh time after time. Pharaoh's heart was hard and he wouldn't listen. When Moses staff turned into a snake, Pharaoh called his magicians. They could do the same thing. Moses told Aaron to take his staff and turn all the water in Egypt into blood. Pharaoh's magicians also turned water to blood. *No big deal*, thought Pharaoh. God made frogs appear everywhere! Pharaoh's magicians did too, making it even worse.

"Moses, pray for the frogs to leave," Pharaoh begged. "Then I'll let you go." But when the frogs died, making a huge stink, Pharaoh changed his mind.

Tiny gnats came and stuck to their skin, got in their hair and their eyes, everywhere. Pharaoh's magicians couldn't copy this. They warned Pharaoh,

"God's power has done it." Pharaoh ignored them. So God sent millions of flies, except in Goshen where the Israelites lived.

Everyone in Egypt had suffered in the plagues. Pharaoh had to do *something*. He said, "Okay. Go and offer your sacrifice to God, but not in the desert. Do it here in Egypt."

"We must leave," Moses said.

"Then go into the desert, but not far." So Moses prayed and the flies left. No surprise—Pharaoh broke his promise again. So God sent a disease that killed almost all the Egyptian animals. But the animals in Goshen were fine.

Each time Pharaoh refused, matters got worse. God sent painful sores that covered the Egyptians and their animals. "No!" said Pharaoh. The worst hailstorm that ever fell in Egypt destroyed every person, animal, and plant that was left outside unprotected—except in Goshen. "No!" said Pharaoh.

Moses warned that grasshoppers would come to eat up every plant the hail had missed, hundreds of thousands of grasshoppers. "Our country is being destroyed!" Pharaoh's officials cried. So Pharaoh bargained with Moses and Aaron, "Go worship. But take only your men."

"We must all go," Moses insisted.

"No! No! NO!" Pharaoh drove Moses and Aaron out of the palace. Then God sent darkness. For three days no

one could see or go anywhere. But Goshen had light.

Pharaoh said, "All right! Go. But leave your animals and flocks."

"No," Moses replied. "We'll need animals to sacrifice to God."

"No way!" Pharaoh yelled. "Get out of my sight! I never want to see you again!"

"All right, I'll go," Moses said. "You'll never see me again." Pharaoh thought he had won. But something inside told him it wasn't over yet.

Questions:

1. Which plague in this story do you think was the worst? Why?
2. God can do anything. If you could have him do something huge and amazing for you, what would it be?

Prayer:

Ask God to help you remember: NOTHING is too big or too small for Him to take care of.

Midnight Wait

(Exodus 11–12)

Joshua watched children scurry along dusty lanes and across small squares as a huge crowd gathered at the edge of town.

"Look," one little girl said, tugging her brother's hand. "Is that Moses?"

The boy looked at two men standing on a pile of straw in the middle of the crowd. It was Moses! He strained to get a glimpse of Moses' famous staff. All the children were curious about the staff God used to work miracles. Joshua laughed softly at the boy's disappointment. Moses staff looked like ordinary wood!

Then Joshua heard Aaron's deep voice rise above the

crowd. "Tonight it will end! The firstborn son in every house in Egypt—from the palace to the jail to the barns—will die. Then Pharaoh will let us go!"

Everyone started talking at once! God had protected His people from the last six plagues. Would He save them from the worst plague of all? Some of the boys were very nervous.

Moses held up his hands for quiet. He spoke calmly, "Don't worry. If you do as God says, our firstborn sons and animals will be safe. Mark your doorframes with lamb's blood to show your family belongs to God."

"Dress ready to go before you eat," Aaron added. "Tonight we leave Egypt."

The crowd cheered. "Come, children," the father of the boy and girl said. "Let's get a lamb for supper."

Joshua hurried home to his own family thinking it was a good thing that the people trusted Moses.

Throughout Goshen, Israelite fathers followed God's instructions. Joshua killed a lamb and drained its blood into a bowl. He gathered his children around him as he dipped a hyssop branch into the blood and wiped it across the top and sides of their doorframe. He made sure the blood was easy to see. "We need to trust God," he told his children. "And we need to believe Moses and Aaron. They've been right about everything else. They're right about this."

Then Joshua's wife built up their fire to cook the lamb, making a flat bread without yeast. While the food

cooked, they packed the most important things for their trip and made sure the animals were fed and watered. As slaves, they didn't have many clothes, but they chose their best and most comfortable. These clothes would have to last until they reached Canaan. The children were so excited. They had never been on a trip before!

Finally, after they ate the roasted lamb, there was nothing to do but wait.

As midnight neared Joshua's firstborn son moved close to him. "Will God's angel see the blood, Dad?" he asked.

"Yes," Joshua answered. "God always keeps His promises."

Suddenly, they began to hear noises in the night: screams, cries, moans, and shouts. The angel of death was passing through every house and every barn in Egypt— except those with blood on their doors!

Just before dawn the word came from Moses. "Pharaoh says we can leave! Go to your Egyptian neighbors and ask them for gifts. God will make them give you whatever you ask for. Let's go!"

Parents and children scrambled to put the last few things in their packs, adding the gifts from their neighbors. "Take it and go away," the Egyptians said. "If you stay, your God will destroy us."

Joshua and his family joined the long, long line leaving Egypt. They weren't slaves anymore! God had freed them! Joshua had been born in Egypt. It was the

only home he had ever known. *What will it be like to travel through the desert?* he wondered.

He glanced at his firstborn son walking beside him. "Just think, Dad. I am alive today because a lamb died and gave his blood to save me," his son said, thoughtful.

"Yes," Joshua agreed. "We will always remember when the angel of death passed over us." To this day, their descendants celebrate that night called the Passover, to remember God's promise.

Questions:

1. What do you think might have happened if some Israelites had not put lamb's blood on their doors?
2. God always knows what the future holds. Why should we follow His instructions?

Prayer:

Thank God for being your loving Father and protecting you even in the midst of danger.

Wind, Waters, and Chariots

(Exodus 13:17–14:31)

Miriam smiled as children raced in and out of the wagons, herds, and people, laughing and teasing. They'd never been so happy! She walked alongside her brother Moses, remembering the day she had put him in a basket in the river. Now Moses was leading the people out of Egypt!

A huge cloud moved ahead of them. At night it became a pillar of fire. God's presence with us, Miriam thought. *The cloud and the pillar of fire show us exactly where to go and remind us we are safe.* "Have you noticed, Moses?" Miriam asked. "It seems God is leading us in circles."

"Yes," Moses answered, glancing back over his shoulder to check the flocks. "I think Pharaoh's army might be following us. God wants to make them think we are lost." He picked up his pace at the thought. "God did say He would show Egypt one final time that He was the true God."

As the sky began turning orange, Moses told the Israelites to set up their tents. They would spend the night here by the Red Sea. Murmurs of alarm went through the camp. "Moses brought us here to die!" someone yelled.

Suddenly, pouring over a hill behind them was the whole Egyptian army: thousands of soldiers and hundreds of chariots. Dust filled the air as far as Miriam could see. They were still far away but the army moved fast! Moses had been right. Pharaoh changed his mind— again. Miriam looked at the sea in front of them. The people were right too. They were trapped!

Was it all for nothing? Miriam wondered. *What will we do now?* A trumpet pierced the growing panic and a hush fell over the crowd. "Stand firm!" Moses shouted. "You'll see how the LORD will save you today. Do you see those Egyptians?" he pointed to the approaching army. The crowd nodded. "You'll never see them again!" Moses yelled. "The LORD will fight for you."

Moses paused to ask God for help and direction. "God will make a way for us," Moses pointed his staff, "through the Sea!"

The cloud of God's presence in front of them moved behind them to block the Egyptian army. A cheer rang out! God was already fighting for them. Moses walked to the edge of the Red Sea and stretched out his hand over it. A strong east wind sprang up, pushing the waters apart. All night the east wind blew with a cloud of fire between the Israelites and their enemies.

In the morning, the Israelites saw the giant walls of water pushed back by the wind. The lake bed was dry! And walls of water lined both sides of the path. The scene was incredible, but they had no time to gawk. There were millions of people to get across to the other side, not to mention all the animals and supplies.

"Hurry. We must hurry," Moses urged.

When the last Israelite reached the other side, they all looked back. The Egyptians were coming after them between the walls of water. But the lead chariots stopped.

"I think their wheels are stuck," someone said.

"God's fighting against them all right!" said another.

Moses stood on a huge rock nearby. He reached his hand out over the Sea.

Suddenly the army panicked. "The waters are coming back!" they screamed. The wind stopped blowing as the waters fell back into the path God had made for the Israelites. The Egyptian chariots and soldiers were flooded. The whole army vanished!

"The LORD will reign for ever and ever!" Miriam jumped in the air and shouted happily. She took a

woman's hand near her and began dancing. Soon many women held hands and danced in a giant wavy line on the beach, celebrating and thanking God. Miriam and her brother Moses sang God's praises until they had no voices left. They had far to go before they would reach the Promised Land of Canaan, but God had saved them again, and now they had the confidence to start.

Questions:

1. Why were the people terrified when they were trapped between the Red Sea and the Egyptian army? Why wasn't Moses afraid?

2. When it looks like there's no way out, how can you be more like Moses than the Israelites?

Prayer:

Ask God to show you what to do when you're in trouble. Be specific. Is a friend mean to you? Need help on a test? Tell God.

Shaky Mountain, Solid Laws

(Exodus 19:1–20:26; 31:18–33:6; 34:1–35)

"M ount Sinai! I used to take Jethro's goats to graze there. And that's where I saw the burning bush," Moses told Aaron and Miriam, pointing to the towering mountain before them. "God said I would come back with all of His people. Now we're here! Wait for me," he said. "I want to go to talk with God on the mountain." A few days later, Moses gathered the elders together. "If you obey God completely," he said, "God says that out of all the nations you'll be His special treasure."

"We will obey!" they cheered.

Then God told Moses, "I'm going to come to you in a thick cloud, and the people will hear me speaking with you. They will always put their trust in you."

So Moses told the people to get ready to meet with God in three days. On the third day, thunder cracked and lightning flashed. The people gathered at the foot of the mountain. Then smoke covered Mount Sinai, because the LORD came down on it in fire. The whole mountain shook. Then Moses spoke. And the voice of God answered.

The people trembled in fear as they saw God's power. They told Moses, "Speak to us yourself. Then we'll listen. But don't let God speak to us or we'll die!"

"Don't be afraid," Moses said. "God wants you to respect Him. That will keep you from sinning."

Then God called Moses back up the mountain to learn more about how to live as His people. Aaron and Hur took charge of the camp. *Surely they won't be gone for long,* Aaron thought, watching Moses and Joshua disappear over the ridge of a hill as they headed for Mount Sinai.

Four weeks passed, then five. Moses and Joshua still weren't back. The people grew restless. "Make a god to lead us," they told Aaron. "Who knows what happened to this fellow Moses." The people wanted a god they could see and control, without thunder, lightning, and awesome power.

Aaron wasn't sure what to do with Moses gone. He forgot to ask God for help and decided to go along with the people. "Bring me your gold earrings," he said.

Aaron melted the gold they brought and shaped it into a calf.

The people said, "Here is our god who brought us

out of Egypt." Then Aaron built an altar and offered sacrifices—before a golden calf! The people had a wild party and turned away from the God who had parted the sea, fed them, and led them safely through the desert.

On the mountain, God told Moses what the people were doing. Moses quickly came down the mountain, carrying two stone tablets. With His own finger, God had written ten commandments on the stone:

"I am the LORD your God. Do not put any other gods in place of Me.

Do not misuse the name of the LORD your God.

Remember to keep the Sabbath day holy.

Honor your father and mother.

Do not commit murder.

Do not commit adultery.

Do not steal.

Do not give false witness against your neighbor.

Do not long for anything that belongs to your neighbor."

These ten rules for living covered every sin of the human heart. It made perfect sense to Moses. If you obeyed the commandments, you would please God—and have a good life!

As Moses and Joshua approached the camp, they saw people out of control and dancing before the calf. They had already broken their promise to follow God! Moses threw the tablets of stone down in anger. They broke into

pieces. "Aaron," he roared, "What's going on?"

Aaron lied, "I threw the gold into the fire and out came this calf!" But even as he said this, Aaron knew that God can't be fooled.

Moses smashed the calf, then told the people, "You've done a terrible thing. But I'll pray. Maybe God will forgive you."

Sin has a terrible price. God forgave the people, but He sent a plague to punish those who weren't sorry for worshipping the calf. Then God wrote the Ten Commandments on new stone tablets for Moses to take with them on their journey.

"I think I'm beginning to get it," Aaron told Moses. "There are two parts to being God's people. We need to obey God; THEN God will bless us, look after us, and take care of our needs."

Questions:

1. Why do you think Aaron let the Israelites make a new god, even though he knew better?
2. Name some ways you can respect your parents (the fifth commandment).

Prayer:

Ask God to help you obey Him instead of going along with the crowd like Aaron.

God's Home

(Exodus 31:1-11; 35:4-36:7; 40:1-38)

Bezalel raced into his tent to find his wife.

"Guess what? We're going to make a tent for God. Moses called it a Tabernacle. God said He would live with us in this special tent and He showed Moses exactly how to build it. Everyone who wants to can bring a special gift. How I'd love to work on it," Bezalel sighed.

His wife smiled fondly. "You're the best craftsman in the camp!" Bezalel grinned. What a privilege it would be! But there were many good craftsmen. Would God choose him?

Bezalel's wife brought her gift to the stockpile for

building the Tabernacle. Stunned by heaps of precious jewels and gold, Bezalel gasped. "Who would have thought ex-slaves would have all this? God's been good to us."

Suddenly a trumpet blast turned everyone's eyes toward Moses. "I have good news," Moses announced. "The LORD has chosen a craftsman to build the Tabernacle. Bezalel, son of Uri, son of Hur, from the tribe of Judah will be in charge. God has also chosen Oholiab, son of Ahisamach, to help Bezalel."

Bezalel's wife grabbed his arm. Bezalel was speechless. God had chosen *him* from all of the craftsmen in the camp!

"God said He has filled Bezalel with His Spirit," Moses added. "We'll build the Tabernacle just as God says. Bezalel, Oholiab, and anyone who wants to help, come see me."

Bezalel suddenly froze. *Can I really do all that?* he questioned. But his wife's face glowed with pride. *If God says I can, then I can,* he decided. Kissing his wife, he ran to Moses.

Soon, the plans were underway. Bezalel and Oholiab learned what each person could do, organized groups, assigned tasks, and made sure everyone knew their job.

All the Israelites were excited. Every day they brought more jewels. Finally the workers told Moses, "We have everything we need." So Moses told the people to stop.

There were many things to make: furniture, embroi-

dered curtains, pillars and poles, tables, and walls for the tent. But Bezalel was the only one skilled enough to build the most important part of all—the ark of the covenant. Moses told him the ark was like God's own seat, and it would hold the stone tablets.

This will be the most beautiful thing I've ever made, Bezalel promised himself. First he formed a box with acacia wood, exactly the size Moses said. Beating gold into paper-thin sheets, he used them to cover the box inside and out, so no wood showed.

Bezalel stood back. It looked good. *Now comes my finest work*, he thought. Bezalel hummed and sang to God as he hammered and chiseled. Patiently for many, many days, he shaped and reshaped the gold cover until he was satisfied.

When he was finally done, Moses came to look, and he couldn't believe what he saw. A golden cherub (beautiful winged creatures around God's throne) sat at each end of the cover. They looked toward the cover with their wings stretched up and over it. "It's amazing!" Moses exclaimed. "It makes me feel close to God just looking at it." That was exactly what Bezalel had hoped.

Finally, he set up the ark of the covenant in the Tabernacle. Aaron and his sons dressed in their priestly robes for the very first time. Moses offered sacrifices to God and used a special spiced oil to anoint the Tabernacle and priests. God told Moses this oil would set apart people and things as holy to God. Everyone

watched in wonder.

Suddenly God's cloud covered the Tabernacle and His glory filled it. The presence was so strong that everyone fell down with their faces to the ground. Even Moses couldn't enter the tent!

Even with his face in the desert sand, Bezalel was filled with joy. "Thank You, God, for letting me work on Your Tent," he prayed. "And for being with us and being our God."

Questions:

1. Name some gifts and talents that people gave to God in this story.
2. What are some gifts and talents you can give to God and to your church?

Prayer:

Thank God for all you have that comes from Him. (Hint: That's *everything!*) Ask for His help to be generous in giving them back to God and to others.

Foolish Scouts

(Numbers 13–14)

The Promised Land! Canaan! Soon it will be ours! Joshua could hardly wait to see it. Moses had called one leader from each of the tribes descended from the sons of Israel: Reuben, Simeon, Judah, Dan, Naphtali, Gad, Asher, Issachar, Zebulun, Manassah, Ephraim, and Benjamin. Joshua, Moses' trusted assistant, was from the tribe of Ephraim.

Moses sent the twelve to see what Canaan was like. "See whether the people who live there are strong or weak, whether they are few or many," he told them. "See how good the soil is there and, if possible, bring back some fruit!"

The men trudged across the dry, scrubby region called the Negeb. Finally they stared across rolling green hills and grinned. The soil looked so rich it seemed anything could grow. They plucked and ate ripe fruit as they walked, letting the juice run down their chins. Fruit! It was delicious! God faithfully gave them manna to eat every day in the desert. They never went hungry, but eating the same food all the time got boring.

"Look at that!" one scout named Shammua exclaimed. A huge walled city covered the next hilltop. "The walls must be the height of eight men," he guessed. "And look. There's nowhere for attacking soldiers to hide from archers. We could never take that city."

Joshua disagreed. "If God is with us, nothing can stand against us."

Others weren't so sure. "Come on," Caleb urged. "Let's see more of our beautiful land." It *was* beautiful, covered with trees and healthy crops. And water! For two years the men had seen little water. Here it looked like it would never dry up.

Caleb noticed tall, muscular men working in a field. "Look at these healthy people," he said. "You can tell they live in a rich land and eat well."

"Too healthy," Palti muttered. "Look how strong they are."

"And tall! They must be descended from the giants," Gaddi added.

After forty days, the scouts returned to camp. On

their way back, they cut off a bunch of grapes so big it took two men to carry it. "It's amazing," Joshua told Moses. "We'd live well there. Look at this fruit."

"But the people are too strong for us," Palti argued. "The cities have high walls and are very big. We even saw giants."

Caleb interrupted. "We should go and take it. God has given it to us."

But the others disagreed. "We are like grasshoppers compared to those men. They'd crush us." The bad news spread through the camp. The people moaned and complained and turned against Moses and Aaron.

Joshua and Caleb insisted that if God was pleased with His people, He would lead them into that land. If God had said it, nothing could save those "giants!" But the people didn't listen and picked up stones to throw at Joshua and Caleb.

Suddenly God's glory appeared to Moses. "How long will these people make fun of Me? How long will they refuse to believe in Me?" God asked.

"Please forgive them," Moses begged.

God said, "I have forgiven them, just as you asked." But everyone who had doubted God would not see the land He promised them. They would wander a year in the desert for every day the scouts were in the land—forty years. But Caleb and Joshua would see the land because they followed God with their whole hearts. The ten other scouts God punished.

When the people saw how serious their sin was they said, "All right, we believe now. We'll go and take the land."

"You won't succeed," Moses warned. "So don't go up. The LORD isn't with you. Your enemies will win the battle over you."

But some men went anyway. They returned to camp, bloody and exhausted. They had lost the battle. Moses led them and the others into the wilderness, back the way they had come. They wandered there forty years, just as God said. Only Joshua and Caleb were still alive. All the people who were older than twenty when they began, died in the desert.

Questions:

1. How big do you think the giants were? What about the grapes?
2. Would you have gone for the grapes and ignored the giants, or been afraid of the giants and missed out on the grapes? Why?

Prayer:

Ask God to help you not be afraid and to listen when you're asked to do something.

Joshua and the Jordan

(Exodus 17:8–16; Deuteronomy 34; Joshua 1, 3–4)

Joshua had known this moment was coming, but he hadn't expected to be so scared. He stood beside Moses in front of all the people. The forty years of wandering was over.

Moses told them, "I'm leaving you now. I won't be entering the Promised Land. Joshua must lead you in." He put his arm across Joshua's shoulders. "Since Joshua was a young man, he's been my assistant. He led you in your first battle against the Amalekites."

The people cheered. Joshua remembered how scared he had been. But as long as Moses held up his hands that day, they had won the battle.

"Joshua waited at the bottom of the mountain when God gave me His laws," Moses added. "He didn't worship the golden calf. He stayed outside the Tabernacle when I talked with God and even when I wasn't there. He loves the LORD."

Moses continued. "Joshua and Caleb were with the leaders who scouted the land forty years ago. Now," Moses' voice boomed, "God has chosen Joshua to be your next leader!"

Joshua was humbled by their cheers. The people respected Joshua, but they didn't want Moses to leave. And neither did he.

Joshua felt the people's eyes on him. *Will they follow me?* he wondered. *Will God be with me as He's been with Moses? Can I please Him as Moses has?*

"God has chosen you," Moses said to Joshua. "He'll guide you and give you all you need."

The next day, Joshua went with Moses to the base of Mt. Nebo. Moses said goodbye and climbed the mountain. No one ever saw him again. The people cried for Moses for a month. He had led them for so long.

Finally, it was time to move on. God said to Joshua, "Be strong and brave. Make sure you obey the whole law my servant Moses gave you. . . Then things will go well with you. And you will have great success. . . I am the LORD your God. I will be with you everywhere you go."

Joshua knew that if they were finally going to conquer the Promised Land, he needed to convince the

people to follow him. His first challenge was to get everyone across the Jordan River. He looked at the rushing, muddy water. It was flood time, and the river was running over its banks. There was no way to cross. *No way without God,* Joshua corrected himself. *God can do anything.*

God told Joshua, "Today I will begin to honor you in the eyes of all of the people of Israel. Then they will know that I am with you, just as I was with Moses."

Joshua told the priests, "Bring the ark of the covenant and stand by the Jordan River." When the priests brought the ark, Joshua told the people, "As soon as the priests step into the Jordan, it will stop flowing. . . . That's how you will know that the living God is among you."

Joshua nodded, and the priests stepped into the waters. *Have I heard God right?* Joshua wondered, holding his breath. Sure enough, the waters stopped flowing down the river. Miles away they piled up near a town called Adam. Soon the riverbed was dry.

Thank you, God, Joshua prayed as the people crossed over. *Now I know that You are with me, too.* He waved twelve men over, one from each tribe. "God back to the middle of the Jordan River. . . . Each one of you must pick up a stone," he said. "The stones will always remind the Israelites of what happened there."

When all the people were across the Jordan, the priests followed with the ark. As soon as they stepped out of the riverbed, the waters started flowing again! That

night they camped in the Promised Land at a place called Gilgal.

"Bring the stones," Joshua told the twelve men. "Pile them here as a memorial." All the people watched. "When your children see these stones and ask what they mean, tell them what God did for you today. Never forget," he said.

The people listened to Joshua because they knew now that God was with him, just as He had been with Moses. Now it was time to go in and take the land.

Questions:

1. Why do you think God chose Joshua to be the next leader?
2. Joshua was a good person and strong leader. What are some ways you can be more like Joshua?

Prayer:

Ask God to help you to be brave like Joshua by staying close to Him.

The Craziest Plan

(Joshua 2, 5:13–6:27; 11:23)

Rahab had heard about the Israelites crossing the desert. Who hadn't? It would be hard to miss more than a million people, not to mention all their flocks and supplies. There were rumors that they were headed toward Jericho, the city where she lived. So she wasn't surprised when one day two suspicious strangers showed up at her house in the wall of the city.

People often gathered at Rahab's house to talk, but there was something different about these two. They seemed to ask a lot of questions. *They must be Israelite spies*, Rahab thought. Unfortunately, she wasn't the only one to guess. Someone who had been listening, hurried out the door.

Quickly, Rahab approached the spies Joshua had sent. "You're in danger," she whispered. "Someone just left to report you to the king of Jericho."

Fear seized them. How did they give themselves away? If they were caught, they would be killed.

"We must leave. Now!" the skinny spy said, starting to rise.

"No. They'll watch the door. Go up those stairs," Rahab nodded to a dark corner. "Hide on the roof and cover up with the flax drying up there. I'll tell you when it's safe."

As they lay in the itchy flax, waiting, they wondered. *Can we trust this woman?* Then Rahab appeared. "I convinced them you'd left," she said, brushing flax off them. "I know your God is powerful. He dried up the Red Sea for you and defeated your enemies. Everyone is afraid of you. Promise me you'll spare my family when you take Jericho."

The spies were amazed that Rahab understood so much about God and His people. "We will," they agreed. "But you must hang a scarlet cord from the window as a signal. And only the people in this house will be safe."

Rahab lowered a rope from her window over the side of the wall and the spies climbed down. After hiding for three days they returned to report to Joshua. They told him about Rahab and how she had saved them.

Vowing to follow God's instructions exactly, Joshua called his army together. "This group," Joshua pointed, "will lead the army ahead of the priests to protect

them. The priests will carry the ark of the covenant while seven priests carry trumpets made from ram's horns. Your group," he pointed to Caleb, "will march behind the priests." Then Joshua explained the rest of God's plan.

The next day Rahab watched as the Israelite army silently marched around Jericho. The only sounds were the tramping of feet, and the clink of armor and weapons as they walked. A scarlet rope hung from her window on the wall, just as she had promised.

After circling the city, the army returned to camp. They did the same thing for five more days. By the fifth day the people of Jericho lined the walls of the city, laughing, pointing, and calling them names. But the Israelites stayed quiet, as Joshua had ordered. This was no ordinary battle plan. It was God's plan!

On the seventh day, the army circled Jericho *seven* times. The priests blew their trumpets as they marched. This time, the people in the city didn't laugh and the walls were empty except for soldiers. Israel's army stopped and faced the city. Then the priests blew one long blast. That was the signal. All of the people gave a loud shout! Imagine the terror inside Jericho when the walls shook and fell flat! The Israelites ran straight in, just as God had said.

Rahab waited nervously at her house. *Will the spies keep their promise to me now?* she wondered. If they didn't, she and her family would surely die. But God remem-

bered her. "Get Rahab and her family. Keep them safe at the edge of the camp." Joshua ordered his men. So that very day Rahab joined God's people as they conquered the land.

Joshua's fame spread and God was with him as he led Israel into the land God had promised to Abraham and his descendents. Then Joshua divided it among the tribes and they all began to use the beautiful land— including Rahab and her family.

Questions:

1. What do you think Israel's soldiers might have thought of God's plan at first?
2. Think of some problem you have. Do you think God might have a different way of solving it than you?

Prayer:

Ask God to help you follow His plans. They work.

Women Win the War

(Judges 2:7, 10–23; 4–5)

Deborah sat under a palm tree, trying to stay cool. *I wish I'd lived in Joshua's day,* she thought. *Then people saw God's wonders with their own eyes.* She sighed. *Now they serve false gods and expect life to go well. When will they learn?*

The Israelites kept making the same mistake over and over. They would stop following God and God allowed their enemies to conquer them so they would understand how sin ruined their lives. When life became unbearable, the people remembered God and cried to Him for help. Then God would raise up a leader (or judge) to defeat their enemies and lead Israel back to God.

The amazing thing, Deborah thought, *is that God keeps helping us and leads us back! Then what do people do? The same thing all over again!* "Please God," she prayed, "Help us. Our enemies have ruled us for twenty years now because we've left You and followed false gods."

Deborah was one of Israel's judges. All day she gave advice to people. *At least they're starting to see that they need God,* she thought hopefully. That evening as Deborah waited for her husband, Lappidoth, to return from the fields, God spoke to her heart. He promised to give the Israelites victory over Jeber and his army commander Sisera. All they had to do was follow God's directions. Immediately, Deborah sent for Barak, the son of Abinoam, to lead the men into battle.

Lappidoth sat down beside her, wiping the sweat from his forehead. "What are you thinking about?" When Deborah told him what God had said, Lappidoth smiled, "Good! God uses you because you trust Him."

By the time Barak arrived, God had given Deborah the battle plan. She said, "Gather 10,000 men at Mount Tabor. God will draw our enemy into a trap. Sisera will bring his chariots and soldiers to the Kishon River. Then God will hand him over to you."

Barak scratched his head. Ten thousand men was a small army against such a terrible foe. And Sisera was a skilled general. Besides, the Canaanites had taken all

their weapons! Ten thousand unarmed, untrained men against Sisera's entire army?

Deborah knew what Barak was thinking. She'd thought it herself. But with God on their side, it didn't matter.

Finally Barak said, "I'll go, *but only* if you go with me."

"All right," Deborah said. "I'll go with you. But because of the way you are doing this, you won't receive any honor. The LORD will hand Sisera over to a woman."

Barak gathered his men at Mount Tabor. When Sisera heard, he brought 900 chariots up the Kishon River valley, just as Deborah had expected. His warrior's chariots thundered up the dry riverbed in record time. Sisera never even saw the black storm cloud gathering behind him.

Deborah smiled at Barak. "Go! You see that coud? Trust the Lord!" So Barak's men marched out. Just then, God opened the cloud and rain streamed down to flood the riverbed Sisera was using as a road. In no time, Sisera's chariots were bogged down in the thick mud. Now the Israelite foot soldiers had the upper hand! The brutal Canaanites panicked and ran, but Barak and his men chased them.

Sisera knew his army was done for. The only thing he could do was escape. Exhausted, He came to Heber's tent and climbed inside. *Heber's my friend. I'll be safe here,* he thought.

Heber's wife Jael greeted him, "Come in. Don't be afraid. Rest here." She gave him milk to drink and let him sleep. But she wasn't being nice to him. She had a secret plan. Jael knew Sisera was Israel's enemy. So when Sisera was asleep, she killed him.

Barak raced up, panting. "Have you seen Sisera? Jael pushed the tent flap aside for Barak to see. Deborah's words had come true: a woman had defeated Sisera.

Deborah told the people, "*God* has beaten our enemies today!" She called them to serve and obey Him again. The Israelites won many more victories after that. They beat the Canaanites so badly that the Canaanites finally gave up. For forty years there was peace in the land.

Questions:
1. Why do you think Barak wanted Deborah to go with him?
2. What kinds of thoughts does God give you while you're relaxing?

Prayer:
Ask God to help you obey Him no matter what.

Gideon Goes with God

(Judges 6–8)

Gideon hid inside a winepress, threshing the grain from his harvest by beating it with a stick. *It sure is stuffy in here*, he thought, wiping his forehead. *But at least I might be able to save some of my grain from the Midianites.* After Deborah died, the people had turned away from God—again. So for seven years God let the cruel Midianites and Amalekites destroy the Israelites' crops and flocks. Now they were very hungry and poor and they called to God for help.

Gideon glanced up, startled to see someone in the winepress with him. (He didn't know it was a messenger from God.) "Mighty warrior, the LORD is with you," the messenger said.

It doesn't look like that to me, Gideon thought to himself. "But the LORD has handed us over to the Midianites," he said aloud.

The messenger said, "You are strong. Go save Israel from them. I am sending you."

"Me?" Gideon scoffed. *"I'm just a nobody."* But God promised to be with Gideon and said he would strike down the Midianites with one blow.

But Gideon wasn't sure. "I need a special sign to know this message is from God," he begged. He brought some food and put it on a rock. When the messenger touched the food with his staff, fire blazed out of the rock and burned it up! Then Gideon *knew* he had seen an angel, and he worshipped God.

It wasn't long before the Midianite and Amalekite armies were back. This time there were more soldiers than anyone could count.

It's time for action, Gideon thought. Beginning boldly, he blew a trumpet to call the Israelites to war. *But what if I'm wrong?* he thought again. *I need another sign!*

"LORD God," he prayed, "Please do something." He looked around. "See this piece of wool? In the morning if there's dew on the wool and nowhere else, I'll know Your promise to use me to save Israel will come true."

Gideon tossed in his bed. I've got to be sure, he worried to himself. Early the next morning he ran to check the wool. It was wet. Everything else was dry! Gideon sighed in relief. But sure enough, he started doubting again. *What if someone poured water on the wool?* he thought.

Gideon prayed again. "Please don't be angry, God. Tonight make the wool dry and everywhere else wet." God is patient. He wasn't angry. He knew Gideon's heart wanted to serve Him. So He did as Gideon asked. In the morning the wool was dry, but the ground was wet with dew. Finally Gideon was *sure*.

As he looked over his rag-tag army of skinny farmers camping near the Midianites, Gideon wondered. *Do we have enough men for the job?*

Immediately, God spoke to Gideon's heart, "You have too many men. They'll think they defeated the enemy themselves. Let everyone who is afraid go home."

Too many? Gideon gasped. But he trusted God and told the men to go home if they were afraid. Gideon watched as first one man, then hundreds, then thousands of men silently took their weapons and left camp. When they were gone, only 10,000 were left.

But God had another idea. He told Gideon to take his men down to the water and watch how they drank. Once again, Gideon obeyed. Most of the men got on their knees and put their faces in the water. A few lifted the water to their mouths keeping their heads up. God told Gideon to keep the few who kept their heads up because good soldiers were always on guard.

Now, only 300 men were left! Gideon shivered. *Truly only God can save us now, he thought.*

That night, God told Gideon if he was afraid to attack, he should first go to the Midianite camp and listen. Gideon was scared silly! So sneaking to the edge of the enemy camp

with his servant, Gideon overheard a soldier talking about a strange dream. "That dream is about Gideon," his friend gasped. "Through him, God will defeat our whole army!"

Gideon looked at his servant in amazement. Their courage soared as they crawled back to their camp. Following God's instructions, Gideon gave every man a trumpet, a torch, and a clay jar to hide the torch. Then they surrounded the enemy camp. "Now!" Gideon signaled with his arm. Every man blew his trumpet, smashed his jar, held his torch high, and SHOUTED as loud as he could.

The terrified Midianites woke up and started swinging their swords. They thought a huge army was attacking. They were so confused they even fought each other as they ran!

Just as God promised, in one blow Israel's torment was over. The Midianites and Amalekites never returned. And Gideon, "the mighty warrior," never had to fight again.

Questions:

1. Think about playing basketball one on one against an NBA superstar. (That's kind of how Gideon felt.) What if God told you you'd win?
2. If you'd been in Gideon's army, would you have stayed? Why or why not? Who really won the battle? Why?

Prayer:

Thank God that He always helps you do what He wants you to do.

152

Take My Sandal, Take Your Wife

(Ruth)

Naomi shifted the bag she carried on her head. It held everything she owned. *I used to have a good home. Now I have nothing,* she thought as she trudged along the path leading from Moab. This was the time of the judges in Israel. Naomi remembered the good years in Bethlehem. But then, everything seemed to go wrong.

First there was the famine. Her husband Elimelech took Naomi and their two sons to Moab to find food. Then, one by one, her husband and sons died: Elimelech, Mahlon, Kilion. *Now the only family left are my son's wives,* she sighed.

The two young women walked beside Naomi, softly crying. They were sorry to see her go back home. She'd been like a mother to them. Now they'd never see her again. Naomi stopped as they came to a crossroads. "This is far enough. Go home to your mothers now," she told Ruth and Orpah. "You've been good to me and to my sons. God will take care of you in your own land." Naomi cried as she kissed them goodbye.

"Why can't we go with you?" Orpah begged. Ruth nodded.

"I have no idea how I'll live in Bethlehem," Naomi warned. "You'll be better off here. Maybe you can get married again." Orpah agreed that was the best idea. But Ruth was firm.

"Don't make me go back there," Ruth begged. "Where you go I'll go. Where you stay I'll stay. Your people will be my people. Your God will be my God." Naomi knew she couldn't change Ruth's mind. So saying one last goodbye to Orpah, they turned toward Bethlehem.

Everyone was glad to see Naomi again but sorry to hear her sad news. Now she was a widow with no money. It'd be hard finding enough to eat. Naomi and Ruth would have to search for kernels of grain left in the fields after the harvest. "I'll go," Ruth said. "I'm younger and stronger. I'll bring whatever I find home to you."

The next day, Ruth returned with a big bag of barley. This was more food than Naomi ever dreamed of. "Where did you go?" she asked Ruth.

"His name is Boaz," Ruth beamed. "He's very kind

and told his workers to watch out for me. He said I could come back anytime because I was taking care of you."

Boaz! Naomi knew him. She smiled to herself. Boaz was a close relative and a godly man. Perhaps he'd be willing to buy Naomi's land and marry Ruth!

One evening near the end of the harvest, Naomi got an idea. "Ruth," she said. "We're going to find you a new home."

After dark, Ruth covered up with her cloak and hid near the threshing floor where Boaz worked. According to Naomi, he'd stay there all night. When Boaz fell asleep by a pile of grain, Ruth crept over and lay down at his feet. She began to doze, when suddenly she heard a voice.

"Who are you?" he asked.

"I'm Ruth," she thought quickly to remember the plan. "You are my family protector. So take good care of me by making me your wife." Her heart pounded. *How could this work? I must be crazy.*

Boaz seemed to understand. "Bless you," he answered. "There's a family protector who is more closely related to you than I. . . . In the morning if he wants to help you, good. Let him help you. But if he doesn't want to, then I'll do it." He let her sleep there and gave Ruth a gift of grain to carry home when it got light.

Naomi swung open the door as Ruth returned. "Tell me everything!" she said. Ruth did, and afterwards, Naomi ran to hide near the city gates so she wouldn't miss what happened next!

Boaz was gathering the town elders as witnesses, when Naomi's closest relative passed by. Naomi watched

from her hiding spot. "Come and sit," Boaz called to him. "Naomi's back, you know. She's selling her husband's land. You can buy it if you want. If you don't, I'm next in line."

The man wanted to buy it. Naomi held her breath.

Boaz added, "There's just one condition. If you buy the land from Naomi, you must also marry her daughter-in-law Ruth from Moab. That's so her husband's name stays with the land."

"Sounds expensive," the man said. And as the tradition dictated, he gave Boaz one of his sandals to show he was giving Boaz his rights to the land. Naomi had seen enough. She ran as fast as she could to tell Ruth the good news. They hugged each other, thanking God for His kindness.

Boaz and Ruth were married. Naomi lived with them and a year later they had a baby boy who they named Obed. Many years would pass before Obed became a grandfather but when he did, his grandson would be Israel's most famous king: David.

Questions:

1. Why do you think Ruth wanted to stay with Naomi?
2. How can you show people you love that they can count on you?

Prayer:

Ask God to help you be loyal like Ruth.

Samuel Meets God

(1 Samuel 1–4)

Many years after leaders like Deborah and Gideon died, Israel continued to go back and forth with God. The problem was that every man thought he knew how to live without God's help. Eli's sons Hophni and Phinehas were like that. They were priests, but they would take the meat from the burnt offering.

So one man reminded them that God wanted them to burn the fat first, then take what they wanted.

But their servant didn't listen. "Give it to me now or I'll take it by force!" he said, grabbing the best pieces. From the temple steps twelve-year-old Samuel shook his head as he watched. He knew this displeased God. Samuel had been living in the temple since he was three. When God had answered his mother Hannah's prayers for a baby, she dedicated Samuel to serve God his whole life. So when he was old enough, she brought him to the temple in Shiloh to live with Eli the priest and his sons.

Priests should teach people the right way, Samuel thought. *Why don't Hophni and Phinehas care what God thinks?* Eli dozed on the stone bench by the temple door. *And why doesn't Eli stop them?* Samuel knew they also sinned in other ways. He felt God's sadness as he ran errands for Eli. "LORD God, help me know what's right," he prayed.

One night Samuel was asleep on his mattress on the temple floor near the ark of the covenant. Suddenly he woke up. Someone had called him! "Must be Eli," he yawned, padding down the hall to Eli's room. "Here I am," he said.

Eli snorted and woke. "I didn't call you."

Samuel shrugged and returned to bed. He was almost asleep when he heard his name again. He returned to Eli. "You called me?"

"Son, I didn't," Eli said. "Go back to bed."

It happened a third time. Samuel went to Eli, puzzled. "I'm here," he said.

Eli sat up. "I didn't call you, Samuel. Go and lie down. If someone calls out to you again, say, 'Speak,

LORD. I'm listening.'" Samuel returned to bed with his heart thumping. *Could God really be calling him?*

"Samuel," the voice said.

Samuel stuttered, "Speak, Lord. I-I'm listening." He felt like someone was standing right there!

God then told Samuel that He was going to punish Eli's family. "I told Eli I would punish his family forever. He knew his sons were sinning. He knew they were making fun of Me. In spite of that, he failed to stop them." Because of this, God promised to cut short Eli's life and no man in his family line would grow old.

In the morning, Samuel opened up the temple as usual. He was afraid to tell Eli what God said. But Eli asked. After listening, Eli said sadly, "He is the LORD. Let Him do what He thinks is best."

As Samuel grew, God often spoke to him. Samuel came to know God's ways—just as he had prayed—and loved Him more than anything. Then Samuel would tell the people what God said. Soon people knew Samuel was God's prophet.

One day Israel's army lost a fight with the Philistines. They went to Shiloh for the ark of the covenant, thinking if the ark were there God would be on their side. Hophni and Phinehas carried the ark to the battlefield. But the army didn't obey God, so God let the Philistines win. The ark was captured and Hophni and Phinehas were killed.

A soldier from the battlefront ran to Shiloh. Worried

about God's ark, Eli waited by the road. "We lost!" the soldier cried. "Both your sons are dead. And the Philistines captured the ark!" When Eli heard about the ark, he fell backward off his chair, broke his neck, and died. God's promise had come true.

Samuel became the new leader of Israel. God was with him and he taught the people God's ways. The people trusted Samuel and he always told them the truth. He was the perfect leader.

Questions:

1. How do you think Samuel heard God's voice? What might it have sounded like? Why?
2. Samuel listened to God. What are some things you can do to listen to God?

Prayer:

Ask God to help you talk to Him about everything. When you've finished talking, wait for a minute to see if something else comes to mind. Pray about that too.

King Saul Serves Himself

(1 Samuel 8, 10:17–26, 13, 15)

Samuel pushed through the noisy crowds. He'd grown up and now he was a leader and a priest. Goats and sheep chomped on grasses and kids played around people's legs. All of Israel was here to get what they wanted: a king. Their excitement made Samuel sad. God told him, "You're not the one they've turned their backs on. I'm the one they don't want as their king."

They think having a king will make life easier, Samuel thought. *They're wrong. A king will make their children soldiers and slaves. He'll demand taxes. He'll take their best fields, vineyards, and olive groves and give them to his helpers. A king would also take their servants and animals. That's what kings do.* Samuel sighed. He'd done his best.

165

They'd have to find out for themselves.

God told Samuel that Saul, son of Kish, from the tribe of Benjamin, was His choice for Israel's first king. Samuel had to admit Saul *looked* like a king: He was handsome, and a head taller than everyone else. But would he be a good king? And where was he? Samuel was ready to anoint him! A priest's anointing set apart a king as God's choice.

"He has hidden himself among the supplies," God said. The people brought Saul out. When Samuel anointed him with oil, the people roared, "Long live the king!"

Samuel watched Saul begin to prove himself a great warrior. Not long after Saul became king, the town of Jabesh Gilead was surrounded by Nahash, king of Ammon's army. If no help came within seven days, Nahash would torture them cruelly. When Saul heard this, God's Spirit came on him. He led his soldiers against Nahash and defeated him!

God gave Saul many other victories. One day, Saul's son, Jonathan, attacked some Philistines in Geba. Other Philistines gathered their armies against Israel. There were too many soldiers to count and 3,000 chariots. Saul would need God's special help to win this battle!

Samuel told Saul, "I'll come and sacrifice burnt offerings and friendship offerings. But you must wait there for seven days until I come to you. Then I'll tell you what to do." God said only priests could offer sacrifices. But the men were scared and started to leave. Saul watched his army get smaller and smaller. On the seventh day, Saul

offered the sacrifices himself. He was tired of waiting and thought he could get God's blessing his own way.

Just as Saul finished, Samuel appeared. "What have you done?" he asked.

"I had to do it," Saul insisted. "The men were leaving. The Philistines were gathering for battle and you weren't here."

Samuel shook his head sadly. "You did a foolish thing. You haven't obeyed the command the LORD your God gave you. . . . Now your kingdom won't last. The LORD has already looked for a man who is dear to His heart. He has appointed him leader of His people. "

Saul continued to do things his own way instead of God's. *God will still bless me,* he thought. *After all, I'm king.* God knew Saul's sinful thoughts. But He loved Israel and gave them victory over their enemies.

Years later, Saul finally wore out God's patience. Samuel told Saul God's battle plan against the Amalekites. "You will win," Samuel said, "But you must destroy everything that belongs to them.'"

God gave Saul victory as He promised. But Saul let their king live and kept the Amalekites' best animals. In fact, his soldiers kept everything that was valuable and only destroyed weak and worthless things. Saul didn't correct them. But God knew and He told Samuel, "I'm sorry I ever made Saul king. He's turned away from Me and disobeyed."

Samuel's heart broke for Saul. He knew God's word was final. *Oh, Saul,* Samuel mourned. *How conceited you've become!* Then he went to tell Saul what God had said.

Saul smiled when he saw Samuel. He had always liked him. This made Samuel even sadder. "God bless you," Saul said. "I've done what you said."

"Then why do I hear the baaing of sheep?" Samuel asked.

"The soldiers kept the animals for a sacrifice," Saul said, avoiding Samuel's eyes. "Oh, uh, and I brought back their king. . . . But we totally destroyed everything else!" His words tumbled out faster, hoping to convince Samuel.

"Stop!" Samuel cried. "God knows what you've done. He wants obedience more than He wants sacrifices. You refused to do what God told you. So God has refused to have you as king. He's given the kingdom to someone better than you."

Until the day Samuel died, he never saw Saul again. He was filled with sorrow because of what Saul had done. And so was God.

Questions:

1. Why did Samuel think having a king for Israel was not a good idea?
2. Are there ever any good reasons for doing things our way instead of God's? Explain.

Prayer:

Ask God to give you patience to do things His way even when it's difficult.

Samuel Anoints a New King

(1 Samuel 16:1–13)

Samuel was old now. Half dozing in the shade of the olive tree near his home in Ramah, he peeked through partly open eyes. There it was again! A head poked up above a hill behind his house. Saul's man? Samuel wondered. *Saul knows that if there's going to be a new king I must anoint him. What will he do? Kill me? Oh, Saul, why did you get so far off track?*

"Samuel," God's voice broke into his thoughts. "How long will you be filled with sorrow because of Saul? . . . Fill your animal horn with olive oil and go on your way. I am sending you to Jesse in Bethlehem. I have chosen one of his sons to be king."

Samuel knew Saul would be suspicious and might even try to kill him if he left home. *How can I get alone with Jesse and his sons?* he wondered. But God had it all worked out.

Samuel took his anointing oil and set out for Bethlehem with a young cow. As he climbed the hill toward Gibeah, Saul's hometown, Samuel prayed for God's protection. Just as Samuel feared, a guard stood where the road split toward Bethlehem.

"Where are you off to, Prophet Samuel?" the guard challenged.

"I've come to offer a sacrifice to the LORD. Want to join me?"

The guard backed off. "Have a good trip." He let Samuel pass and at the top of the next hill, Samuel looked back and sighed with relief. The guard was gone. No one had followed him.

Samuel and his cow reached Bethlehem in late afternoon. News had traveled fast. The town elders came to meet him. They looked scared. "Have you come in peace?" they asked nervously. Everyone knew that Saul had been watching Samuel and they didn't want any trouble.

"I've come to offer a sacrifice to God. Come and join me." Samuel assured them. "And please invite Jesse son of Obed and his sons."

As people gathered, Samuel prepared for the sacrifice. Jesse was there with seven sons. At once Samuel

noticed Eliab, Jesse's eldest son. He was tall and handsome, with the look of a warrior. *Eliab must be the one God wants me to anoint for Him*, Samuel thought.

But God said, "Don't consider how handsome or tall he is. I have not chosen him. I do not look at the things people look at. Man looks at how someone appears on the outside. But I look at what is in the heart." Samuel thought of Saul. He was tall and handsome, a man who stood out in a crowd. But his looks hadn't made him a good king.

Jesse called Abinadab over to meet Samuel. But the LORD said "Not him." Then Shammah. "No." Five more sons paraded before Samuel. "No. No. No. No. No," God said each time. Samuel was puzzled. Had he misunderstood what God said?

"Are these the only sons you have?" he asked Jesse.

"My youngest son is taking care of the sheep," Jesse answered.

"Send for him," Samuel said. "We won't sit down to eat until he arrives."

Samuel smiled when David arrived from the fields. "Get up and anoint him," God said. "He is the one."

"Get down on your knees, David," Samuel said. He lifted his animal horn and poured oil over David's head until it ran down his hair and onto his face. The Spirit of the LORD came on David with power from that day on. His father and brothers couldn't believe it. David? A king?

The next morning Samuel went home to Ramah. And David? He returned to his sheep. But God was training David to become Israel's greatest king ever. He loved God and did things God's way. Not only would David's family rule Israel. The Messiah—the God-King who would "crush the serpent's head" and repair mankind's relationship with God—would be one of David's descendants.

Questions:

1. What was God looking at when He chose David as king?
2. Do you choose your friends by what's inside or what's outside?

Prayer:

Ask God to help you choose your friends by their hearts and nothing else.

Who Dares Insult God?

(1 Samuel 17)

I'd better hurry if I want to see my brothers, David thought. He led his donkey to the supply tent and unloaded the grain, bread, and cheese his father had sent. His eyes widened in excitement watching Israelite soldiers line up for battle. As David tethered his donkey, Saul's warriors rattled their spears, banged their shields, and shouted to frighten the enemy.

David ran through the lines of men until he found his older brothers Eliab, Abinadab, and Shammah. "I brought you some food," he said. "And Dad said not to worry about the sheep. I've been taking care of them." His brothers tousled his hair and started to tease David when a sudden hush fell over the camp.

David looked up. Somebody from the Philistine army was walking into the valley below them. Either David's eyes were playing tricks on him or the man was enormous! His bronze helmet and armor caught the morning sun like diamonds as he waved a huge spear and a sword as long as David's leg! The man carrying the giant Goliath's shield looked like a kid beside him.

Where had this man come from? And what did he want?

From the center of the valley Goliath yelled, "Send someone to fight me, you dogs! If he wins, we'll be your slaves. If I win, you'll be ours!" The Philistine army roared their challenge.

David was angry. "Goliath is bringing shame on Israel," he said. "He dares the armies of the living God to fight him. Who does he think he is?"

A soldier grunted, "For forty days he's done this. King Saul will make whoever kills him wealthy. He's offered his daughter for a wife and the man's family will never pay taxes. But no one's willing to risk it."

David couldn't believe it. "*I'll* go out and fight him!"

Soon someone tapped David on the shoulder. He turned to face a stern soldier. "The king wants to see you," he said and led David to King Saul's tent.

David bowed low. To think he was in the presence of Israel's king! Then his anger returned when he remembered Goliath shaking his spear. "Don't let anyone

lose hope because of that Philistine," he urged Saul. "I'll go out and fight him."

"You're too young," the king replied. "He's been a fighting man ever since he was a boy."

"I guard my father's sheep," David said boldly. "Sometimes a lion or a bear would come and carry off a sheep from the flock. Then I would go after it and hit it. . . . The Lord saved me from the paw of the lion. He saved me from the paw of the bear. And He'll save me from the powerful hand of this Philistine too."

Saul thought he must be crazy but he offered David his armor. Saul was a big man and the armor was heavy. David felt ridiculous. "I can't go out there in all of this armor," he said. "I'm not used to it." So he took it off. Then he picked up his shepherd's staff and went out to get ready for battle.

David found five smooth stones and put them in his pouch. Taking out the sling he carried to protect his father's sheep, he walked toward Goliath.

Goliath saw how young and small David was and began to rage. "Why are you coming against me with sticks? Do you think I'm a dog? Come over here. I'll feed your body to the birds of the air!" Then he cursed David in the name of his god.

David knew Goliath's god was powerless, so he ignored the curses. "You are coming to fight against me with a spear and a javelin," he shouted. "But I'm coming against you in the name of the LORD who rules over all. . . .

He's the one you have dared to fight against. . . . He will hand all of you over to us."

Goliath roared and charged. David loaded his sling as he ran toward Goliath, whirled it around his head, then slung it with all his might. The stone pounded Goliath's forehead! With a look of surprise, Goliath sank to his knees then dropped, lifeless. With a roar, Israel's army poured down the hill. The Philistines ran!

God fought for Israel that day, just as David knew He would. It was a great victory. When quiet returned to the valley, Saul called for David. "Whose son are you?"

"I'm the son of Jesse from Bethlehem," he said. Soon Saul would know exactly who David was and what God planned for his life.

Questions:

1. Why wasn't David afraid, even though grown men were?
2. What makes you afraid? Why? What can help you be confident like David?

Prayer:

Talk to God about some things you named that make you afraid. Ask Him to help you trust Him like David.

David Sings
to God

(Psalm 23:1-4; 3:1, 3-5; 18:1-3; 63:1,3; 103:1, 5; 34:1-2, 8-9, 18; 56:3-4; 51:9-10; 139:1, 13, 16-17)

Tell me stories about the old days, Dad," Solomon begged. King David pulled Solomon on to his lap. They both loved this bedtime routine. *Life seems so short,* thought David.

There's so much to learn about God and being king! thought Solomon.

"Tell me about when Samuel anointed you." Solomon squirmed with excitement as David smiled and told his son about coming from the pastures to kneel before Samuel.

"I thought there was no way I could become king. But God did it," David said.

"And sing the song about the shepherd," Solomon coaxed. "That's one of my favorites." Solomon jumped down to get the harp. David softly stroked the strings and sang:

> "The LORD is my shepherd. He gives me everything
> I need.
> He lets me lie down in fields of green grass. He leads me
> beside quiet waters.
> He gives me new strength. He guides me in the right paths
> for the honor of His name.
> Even though I walk through the darkest valley, I will not
> be afraid.
> You are with me. Your shepherd's rod and staff comfort me."

David put down the harp and continued his story. "Saul was jealous. He knew God was going to take the kingdom from him and give it to me and my family. Saul thought if he killed me, he could stop God's plan. I ran for my life, even hiding in caves. But God always saved me—from Saul and many other enemies! Then I would write a song telling God how I felt."

"That's one of my favorites," Solomon said. David began singing even before Solomon asked:

> "LORD, I have so many enemies!
> You're like a shield that keeps me safe.
> You help me win the battle.
> "I call out to the LORD. He answers me from His holy hill.
> I lie down and sleep.
> I wake up again, because the LORD takes care of me.
> I love You, LORD. You give me strength.
> The LORD is my rock and my fort.
> He is worthy of praise."

David told Solomon of the times when he and his men traveled for miles without water. When they found a spring, the water refreshed them and gave them energy. "Just as God does," he explained. "Sitting in the shade of a palm tree, I wrote one of your favorites":

"God, you are my God. I greatly long for You.
With all my heart I thirst for You in this dry desert
where there isn't any water.
Your love is better than life. Deep down inside me,
I will praise Him.
He satisfies me with the good things I long for.
Then I feel young and strong again, just like an eagle."

"You see," David said looking into Solomon's eyes, "worship is just talking honestly with God. Thank Him for His goodness. Trust Him when you can't see any way out." David had lots of trouble, but God *always* came through.

"Sometimes I thought I would just burst with love for God," David exclaimed.

"Like the time you danced before the ark, Dad?"

"Like the time I danced before the ark." They both knew the next song! Solomon joined David as they danced around the room:

"I will thank the LORD at all times.
My lips will always praise Him.
Let those who are hurting hear and be joyful.
Taste and see that the LORD is good."

David looked fondly at his son blinking and

yawning to fight off sleep. Soon Solomon would crawl under the covers and say his prayers. "Now sing about how God knows and loves me," Solomon said, snuggling closer as his dad, King of Israel sang in a whisper:

"LORD, *You have seen what is in my heart.*
You know all about me.
You created the deepest parts of my being.
You put me together inside my mother's body.
You planned how many days I would live.
God, Your thoughts about me are priceless.
No one can possibly add them all up."

Then he kissed Solomon good night. David's songs helped Solomon talk to God. If Solomon understood God's love and loved God from his heart, David knew someday he would make a great king!

Questions:

1. Why do you think David told God how he felt if God already knew?

2. When something bothers you or makes you happy do you tell God? Why?

Prayer:

If you want, you can pray a psalm to God like David did: Tell Him how you feel. Then thank Him and tell Him you trust Him.

Solomon Chooses Wisely

(1 Kings 1–4, 10)

Solomon watched from his balcony as his handsome brother Adonijah climbed into his bronze and gold chariot. *He's off to convince the people to make him king*, Solomon thought. *Doesn't he know God chooses kings?*

Then movement in the garden below caught his eye. His mother and the prophet Nathan had been talking. Now Bathsheba nodded and headed toward King David's room. A minute later, Nathan followed.

Solomon guessed what they were up to. Long ago, David had promised Bathsheba that Solomon would be king. They'd gone to remind David. Suddenly Solomon felt cold all over. *Me? King of Israel? How could I ever fill my father's shoes?*

He was still wondering when Nathan bustled in with servants. They dressed Solomon in his finest robes and brought him his father's royal mule. *A sure sign that father has chosen me to be king after him*, Solomon gasped.

Everyone around the palace sprang into action. Zadok the priest brought anointing oil. Benaiah, commander of the king's special guard, signaled his men to guard Solomon as they set off for the Gihon spring. All Jerusalem knew something important was going on and followed them.

"Long live King Solomon!" the crowd roared, as Zadok anointed Solomon with oil and another priest blew a trumpet. Shouting and playing flutes, the people followed Solomon back to the city. Their celebration was so loud the ground shook! And those who had tried to make Adonijah king ran away.

Solomon couldn't believe it, but now he was King! LORD, *help me obey You as my father David taught me*, he prayed. To show God how much he wanted to follow Him, Solomon offered 1,000 sacrifices.

That night Solomon had a dream. In it, God said, "Ask for anything you want Me to give you."

Solomon already knew being king was difficult. There was so much to do, so much to learn! He told God, "You've been very kind to my father David, your servant. That's because he was faithful to you. He did what was right. . . . You have now made me king. But I'm only a

little child . . . . Give me a heart that understands. Then I can rule over your people. I can tell the difference between what is right and what is wrong."

God liked Solomon's answer. He said, "I will give it to you. I will give you a wise and understanding heart. . . . And that is not all. I will give you what you have not asked for. I will give you riches and honor. As long as you live, no other king will be as great as you are. Live the way I want you to. Obey my laws and commands, just as your father David did. Then I will let you live for a long time."

Solomon woke up. He *knew* God would give him everything he needed to be a wise king.

He didn't have to wait long for his first test. One day, two women came to him with a baby. They had been fighting and wanted Solomon to settle their argument.

"We both had sons," the tall woman said. "This woman's baby died. While I was asleep, she took my baby. When I woke up, I thought it was my son who died.

The shorter woman broke in, "No. This baby is mine."

"Bring me a sword," King Solomon told a guard. "Cut the living child in two. Give half to one woman and half to the other." Every head in the palace turned to watch the drama. Would Solomon really do it?

One woman said, "Go ahead. If I can't have him, no one will!"

"No!" screamed the tall woman. "Don't kill him! Give the baby to her, but let him live!"

"Stop!" Solomon shouted. Give the living baby to the first woman. Don't kill him. She's his mother," Solomon said. He knew no mother would allow her baby to be cut in two. He handed the baby to the second woman. "Here is your child." The news of his wise decision spread: God was with Solomon, giving him wisdom to rule his people.

Solomon had thousands of chariots and horses. He built a gorgeous palace and a throne of gold and ivory. Solomon was richer than any other king, just as God had promised. He also knew a lot about plants, animals, birds, reptiles, and fish. He wrote 3,000 proverbs or wise sayings and 1,005 songs. The kings of all the nations heard about Solomon's wisdom and sent their people to learn from him.

Questions:

1. What was the difference between Adonijah's and Solomon's understanding about becoming king?

2. What are some things that you need wisdom for? (Getting along with others? Doing well in school?) Where can you get it?

Prayer:

Ask God for wisdom for the things you listed, for today and every day.

Another House for God!

(1 Kings 5–6, 7:13–9:9; 1 Chronicles 22)

Clang! Thunk! Crack! Mallets struck chisels. Stone cracked apart. Axes chopped logs. The quarry rang with the sound of hundreds of men working. Dust filled the air and turned men's sweat dusty white.

King Solomon watched as two men split a rock in two. He was fascinated. Hammering chisels into the rock, they forced wood wedges into the crack. When they poured water on the wood, it swelled up and pushed the stone apart until it cracked. One block of stone became two!

Other men chiseled the stone into blocks exactly the

right shape and size. Carpenters cut cedar logs into planks. Craftsmen carved palm trees, flowers, and winged angels into wood and stone.

God will finally have a house with us! Solomon thought. *My father's dream will come true.* He remembered what David had told him: "I wanted to build a house for God. But God said I'd fought too many wars. He told me, 'Your son will be a man of peace. He'll build Me a house.'"

King David gave Solomon plans for the Temple and all the things it would need. He gathered gold, silver, bronze, iron, wood, and stone for the work. Most importantly, he gave Solomon his blessing.

Imagine building a house for God, Solomon thought. The Temple was a huge project, and so important it made him tremble. *How can I get it just right? Anything I do will be poor compared to everything God made for us!* He would have to try.

Solomon went to the Temple site in Jerusalem. Here were no clangs, bangs, or cracks—only men's voices and the groaning of oxen. Solomon wanted this to be holy ground right from the beginning.

The Temple walls towered seven times taller than Solomon as he walked between two huge bronze pillars to see the Most Holy Place. There, men covered the stone walls with cedar planks. Solomon breathed in the fresh smell of the wood. *This is a beautiful place,* the king thought. Stone sparkled as the sun shone through the

partly built roof. *I hope God is pleased.*

Solomon often checked the progress on the Temple. After the craftsmen covered all the stone with carved cedar, they carefully pressed thin sheets of hammered gold into the wood to cover the carvings perfectly.

Huram, the bronze expert, proudly showed the king his work. "This mould is for the bronze sea." He nodded at a great clay basin heating in the fire. They called the bowl a "sea" because it was so huge. It would hold water for the priests to wash in when they served in the Temple.

Building the temple was hard work and took a long time, seven years from start to finish. Solomon was so excited. *It was worth every minute!* he thought. *Now it is ready for God to come and live with us!*

Solomon called all Israel together to dedicate the Temple to God. The priests brought the ark of the covenant into the Most Holy Place and placed it under the wings of two gold-covered cherubim. When the priests left the Holy Place, the cloud of God filled the Temple! His wonderful presence was so strong that the priests couldn't continue!

Solomon offered sacrifices and knelt before God's altar. "Dear God, You've been so good to us," he prayed. "There is no God like You. All the heavens can't hold You. So this temple I've built won't hold You. But please listen to Your people's prayers for this Temple. Listen and answer. You are our LORD and King."

God answered, "I have heard you pray to Me. I have heard you ask Me to show you My favor. You have built this temple. I have set it apart for Myself. My name will be there forever. My eyes and my heart will always be there." God had met with Israel in the desert in a tent. Now He would meet with them in a beautiful temple. But He wanted them to understand His laws were still the same—in a tent or in a temple.

The people were thrilled to have a place to worship God. They celebrated for a whole week!

Questions:

1. Do you think Solomon ever felt he couldn't finish such a huge project? Or that it was too important for him? What do you think he did when he felt that way?
2. What are you learning, doing, or trying to change that seems too hard? (God can give you wisdom and strength like he did Solomon.)

Prayer:

Ask God to help you finish things you need to do and to give you the strength and wisdom it takes.

Wise and Foolish Solomon

(1 Kings 11; Proverbs 27:14; 1:7; 2:4, 3, 9; 3:5-6, 11-12; 12:18; 27:17; 4:23; 11:24; 12:22; 14:23; 17:17)

Good morning!" Rehoboam's tutor grinned as the young prince stumbled into the classroom.

"Blessing your neighbor loudly in the morning is like calling down a curse on him," Rehoboam grumped. "That's what my father the king says. Besides, I don't want to study today. I want to go to father's gardens and learn about animals." He hoped his teacher would let him and his brothers go. The palace gardens were full of interesting things!

"If you really want to gain knowledge, you must begin by having respect for the LORD. Foolish people hate wisdom and training," Rehoboam heard his father solomon's voice say. His father always turned up at the wrong time.

"Why do you always talk about wisdom?" he pouted. "It's just words. I'd rather ride my horses or search for hidden treasure or something."

"You'd be better off searching for wisdom the way you search for hidden treasure," Solomon smiled. "You should cry out for understanding and the ability to be wise. Wisdom helps you know what's right, honest, and fair.

"But," Solomon added, "you're right. Having wisdom isn't enough. If you don't *act* wisely, you're still foolish. Wisdom tells you the right way to *live*. I want you to know God's wisdom," he added. "I wrote it down as proverbs for you to study because doing things God's way leads to good lives. God made everything, after all: He knows how it's made to work!"

Rehoboam pouted but he knew Solomon wanted all his children to love wisdom and God. "Trust in the LORD with all your heart," Solomon urged. "Don't depend on your own understanding. In all your ways remember Him. Then He'll make your paths smooth and straight."

Rehoboam sighed and went back to his studies. He wanted a good life, but something inside him also wanted to disobey. "Discipline is for your sake—it helps make you wise and shows you my love," Solomon often said. "It's like God's training. God trains those He's pleased with. Don't hate the LORD's training or object when He corrects you. He trains those He loves."

I'm special, Reheboam thought. *After all, I'm a prince!* But when he was mean to others, Solomon sat him down. "Listen, son. Thoughtless words cut like a sword. But the tongue of wise people brings healing." Glancing at some bad friends Rehoboam hung out with, Solomon added, "Choose your companions carefully. One person sharpens another as iron sharpens iron. But above everything else, guard your heart. It's where your life comes from."

Solomon taught Reheboam wisdom every chance he got. When he asked, "Why should I give any of my money away?" Solomon answered, "Don't love money. Some people give freely but get even richer. Others don't give what they should but get poorer." And lying made Solomon mad! "The LORD hates those whose lips tell lies," Solomon warned. "But He's pleased with people who tell the truth." Solomon urged Reheboam to work hard: "All hard work pays off. But if all you do is talk, you'll be poor." And to be a faithful friend: "A friend loves at all times. He's there to help when trouble comes."

Reheboam was very blessed to have such a wise father. But as he got older, Reheboam noticed that his father was not always acting wisely. In fact, Solomon stopped choosing God's way every day in everything, big or little. Reheboam watched the wise decisions of Solomon's youth fade away when he ignored God's laws.

Solomon's biggest mistake was marrying wives from other lands. God had warned His people not to do that.

He knew that it would cause them to fall away from Him. That is exactly what happened. Solomon's wives begged him to build altars to their false gods. And he did. He even worshiped their false gods with them!

God was angry. He allowed Solomon's enemies to have power over him. God finally told Solomon that because of his sin, He would tear the kingdom away from him and give it to one of his officials. Reheboam should have learned from his father's mistakes and heeded God's warning. He should have asked God to discipline him and train him to be wise. But instead Rehoboam—Israel's next king—began making wrong choices too.

Questions:

1. Which proverb in this story do you like the best? Why?
2. How can you learn wisdom?

Prayer:

Ask for God's help to use the wisdom He teaches you by making right choices every day.

The Kingdom Is Torn Apart

(1 Kings 12; 2 Chronicles 10-11; Proverbs 20:28; 29:4)

As the sun hid behind a cloud, the prophet Ahijah shivered. But he was more afraid than cold. Soon Jeroboam, an important young man in Solomon's court, would arrive on his way out of Jerusalem. Ahijah had a message from God for him. *This is dangerous,* Ahijah thought. *If Solomon finds out that I have met with Jeroboam about becoming the king of Israel, I'm in trouble! But I must obey God over Solomon.*

As Jeroboam appeared, Ahijah got ready to deliver God's message. He took off his new cloak and tore it into 12 pieces. He was acting out what God had told him. Then he called Jeroboam to meet him at the side of the road.

"Take ten pieces," Ahijah told Jeroboam, offering Jeroboam his torn cloak. "God told me that He will tear the kingdom out of Solomon's hands and He will make you king over Israel. He'll give you ten tribes and leave one for David's family. The people have deserted Him and worship false gods. But if you follow God commands, He will be with you, and your family will rule as long as David's."

As soon as Solomon heard the prophecy about Jeroboam becoming king, he sprang into action—not to tell God he was sorry, but to try to kill Jeroboam and stop God's plan. So Jeroboam ran for his life to Egypt. When Solomon died, after reigning as Israel's king for 40 years, Jeroboam returned to Israel.

Meanwhile, the people gathered at Shechem to crown Solomon's son Rehoboam as the new king. Looking through the crowd, Ahijah noticed Jeroboam talking with some leaders. *Jeroboam's back from Egypt!* he thought. *I wonder when God will give him the kingdom?*

Jeroboam approached Rehoboam to speak for the people. "Sir, your father Solomon made us work like slaves in the mines building many fortresses for him. Make our load lighter and we'll serve you."

Rehoboam seemed offended. He was more interested in his own power than what the people needed. So he stalled. "I'll give you my answer in three days," he said.

He has three days to come to his senses, Ahijah thought.

He followed King Rehoboam and his officials to see what they would do. After dinner that night, Rehoboam spoke to the elders who'd served his father for years. "You heard what the people said. What's your advice?"

Good idea, Ahijah thought. *Those old men are wise from their years with Solomon.*

"Serve the people today," the elders said. "Give them what they ask and they'll always serve you. Your father often said, 'Love and truth keep a king safe. Faithful love makes his throne secure.' He also said, 'By doing what's fair, a king makes a country secure.'"

The young men Rehoboam grew up with chuckled. "Solomon didn't follow his own advice, did he?"

Rehoboam turned to them. "Well, then. How about you? What's your advice?"

"Tell them," one said boldly, "that you are much stronger than your father. Say that your father put a heavy load on them but your load will be heavier! He beat them with whips. You'll beat them with bigger whips." The other young men cheered.

The people won't put up with that! Ahijah thought. If Rehoboam followed this advice, God would take the kingdom away from him and Jeroboam would soon be king.

Three days later, the people returned for Rehoboam's answer to Jeroboam's offer. "I'm far stronger than my father," he roared. "His load was heavy. Mine will be worse!"

The people groaned. They realized Rehoboam wouldn't listen to them. "We don't have any share with

David's house," they shouted. That very day, the people denounced his Kingdom.

Ahijah sighed. *It's just as God had said*, he thought. *Nevertheless, it's sad. Solomon and his descendents could have been great kings if only they had listened to God as David had.*

Rehoboam turned white and stumbled from the platform. This wasn't supposed to happen. Wasn't he the *king?* Then he went out with one of his officials to force the people back to work. But the people stoned his official and Rehoboam barely escaped by charging off in his chariot!

The people of Israel made Jeroboam their king just as God had said. Rehoboam remained king of Judah. But that meant that now Israel was no longer one kingdom, but two. It had lost the peace and glory of Solomon's reign, and divided into jealous, bickering tribes.

Questions:

1. Some counselors gave Rehoboam wisdom, some gave their opinion. Which do you think is which? Why?
2. If Rehoboam had asked you for advice, what would you have said? Why?

Prayers:

Thank God for giving you people like your parents to teach you wisdom. Ask God's help to know the difference between His wisdom and people's opinions.

Famine Ends with Fire

(1 Kings 17–20, 21; 2 Kings 2)

Ever since Jeroboam, the kings of Israel had refused to serve and follow God. God sent prophets as messengers to call His people back to Himself, but few listened. King Ahab and Queen Jezebel were the most evil rulers Israel ever had. Queen Jezebel fed the prophets of the false gods. But she *killed* God's prophets.

One prophet of God, Elijah, walked into King Ahab's palace. "I serve the Lord. He is the God of Israel. You can be sure that He lives. And you can be just as sure that there won't be any dew or rain on the whole land. There won't be any during the next few years. It won't come until I say so," he said. Then God told Elijah to hide in the desert.

"Caw! Caw!" a bird's cry woke Elijah from his sleep the

next day. *What was this?* A raven dropped bread and meat for him! Twice a day God sent ravens to bring food to Elijah and he drank water from a nearby brook until it dried up from lack of rain. *Time to move on,* he thought. *But where?*

"Go right away to Zarephath," God said. "I have commanded a widow in that place to supply you with food," God said.

A widow? How can a poor widow have enough to feed me in a land is gripped by famine? Elijah wondered. But when Elijah reached Zarephath, he saw a poor woman gathering twigs. *She must be the one God meant,* he thought. "Please bring me water to drink," he said to her. "And bread."

"I have no bread," the woman explained. "I've been gathering twigs for a fire to cook the last meal for my son and I. Then we'll die." Her face was sad and her body bent by work. Life had been hard even before the famine. Now, she had lost all hope.

But Elijah knew God had a different plan for her. "Don't be afraid," he comforted her. "First make a little bread for me. Make it out of what you have. Bring it to me. The LORD is the God of Israel. He says, 'The jar of flour will not be used up. The jug will always have oil in it. You will have flour and oil until the day the LORD sends rain on the land.'" The woman stared at him in wonder, but did exactly as he said. And for three years, her almost empty jars of oil and flour never ran out! They always had food!

Then one day, the woman's son got very sick and died. Elijah cried out to God. "Oh LORD, give this boy's

life back to him!" When the boy sat up, Elijah laughed joyfully. "Look!" he told the widow. "Your son is alive!"

"Now I know that you are a man of God!" she exclaimed.

By now, three years had passed without rain. God told Elijah to go to King Ahab. "Then I will send rain on the land," He promised. So Elijah came out of hiding and returned to King Ahab. "Send for people from all over Israel. Tell them to meet me on Mount Carmel. And bring the 450 prophets of the god Baal," Elijah challenged Ahab. "Let's see whose God is real."

Soon Baal's false prophets and the people of Israel gathered at Mount Carmel. The stage was set. Elijah said, "If the LORD is the one and only God, follow Him. But if Baal is the one and only God, follow him."

The people just stared. *What is he talking about?* they wondered.

"Get two bulls for us," Elijah ordered. "Let Baal's prophets choose one for themselves. Let them cut it into pieces. The let them put it on the wood. But don't let them set fire to it. I'll prepare the other bull. I'll put it on the wood. But I won't set fire to it. Then you pray to your god. And I'll pray to the LORD. The god who answers by sending fire down is the one and only God."

Baal's prophets prepared their bull. Then they prayed to Baal for fire. Nothing happened. All morning they shouted and even cut themselves to get Baal's attention. Nothing. At noon Elijah teased, "Shout louder. Maybe Baal is sleeping. You might have to wake him up." Still

nothing, all afternoon.

In the evening, Elijah prepared his bull and placed it on the wood. Then he dug a ditch around the altar and told the people to pour water on the wood, three times. Everything was soaked and the ditch was full of water.

Elijah prayed simply: "Answer me, LORD, answer me. Then these people will know that You are the one and only God."

Instantly the fire of God fell from heaven and burned up the sacrifice. It even burned up the stones and licked up all the water in the ditch! The people fell on their faces, crying, "The LORD is the one and only God!"

That night God sent rain again, just as He'd promised.

It would be wonderful to say that all the people believed and obeyed God after they saw His awesome display of power. But they didn't. Elijah spent his whole life as God's prophet, trying to call the kings and people of Israel back to God. But they were stubborn and refused to listen.

Questions:

1. Which was your favorite miracle in this story? Why?
2. God can do big and small miracles to work things out for us. Do you think there's anything God can't do? Why or why not?

Prayer:

Thank God for being so powerful. Ask for help to trust Him to do big things in your life.

Stubborn Jonah, Sorry Nineveh

(Jonah)

The storm came out of nowhere! Huge waves crashed against the ship. Soon it would break apart! The sailors cried out to their gods for help and threw precious cargo overboard. If they made the ship lighter, maybe it wouldn't sink.

Captain Ahazel scrambled below deck looking for things to throw overboard. In the gloom, he tripped over a man wrapped in a cloak, fast asleep! Ahazel shook the man. "How can you sleep?" he shouted over the din. "Get up! Call on your god for help. Maybe he'll pay attention to what's happening to us. Then we won't die." Ahazel grabbed the man's arm. He dragged him up to the wildly tilting deck where the sailors crouched in fear.

"Let's throw dice to see whose fault this is," Bediah yelled to the other sailors.

The dice chose the stranger—Jonah. "What terrible thing have you done to bring all of this trouble on us?" Ahazel shouted. "Who are you?"

"I'm Jonah, a Hebrew. I worship the LORD. He is the God of heaven. He made the sea and the land," he answered.

Jonah remembered the day God had told him to go to Nineveh and preach. Prophets say what God tells them to say—that's their job. But Jonah was a prophet with an attitude. He hates the Ninevites. *This time, I'm not going to do what God says*, he thought. *The Ninevites are cruel enemies of the Hebrews. They don't deserve God's mercy.*

So Jonah began to run in the opposite direction. That was why he was on this ship, and why God had sent this horrible storm. The sailors were right. He *was* to blame. "Throw me into the sea," Jonah said to Ahazel. "Then it will become calm."

The sailors tried to row to safety to save Jonah's life, but the storm just got worse. Finally, they heaved him overboard. The stormy sea became calm! When the sailors realized they were saved, they worshiped Jonah's God.

But Jonah was in deep water! First he dog-paddled, then treaded water to stay afloat. Finally, he began to sink—down, down, down. Seaweed wrapped all around him. *I guess I'm done for*, he thought. Just then, a huge fish swooped by and swallowed him. Now God had Jonah's full

attention! For three days and nights, Jonah was squashed inside the fish. But instead of complaining, he worshipped God, thanked Him for saving him, and promised to obey.

Suddenly, the fish spit Jonah onto dry land. Again God told Jonah, "Go to Nineveh and give them my message." This time Jonah obeyed God, but he still didn't like it.

Nineveh was a large city. Jonah stared up at its towering walls. Its noise and smells tumbled over him. Walking through the city, Jonah announced, "In 40 days Nineveh will be destroyed." When he thought about it, he hoped it was true.

But the very first day people heard Jonah, they believed God's warning. The king of Nineveh commanded, "Everyone, including animals, must stop eating and drinking! Wear black clothes to show you're sorry. Call out to God with all your hearts. Stop doing evil and don't harm others. Who knows? Maybe God will have pity on us so we don't die."

When Jonah saw that the people listened to God, he was *really* upset. He didn't want God to save his enemies! "LORD," he complained, "isn't this exactly what I thought would happen when I was still at home? That's why I was so quick to run away. . . . I knew that You are gracious. You are tender and kind. You are slow to get angry. You are full of love. You are a God who takes pity on people. You don't want to destroy them. LORD, take away my life. I'd rather die than live." Jonah hated Nineveh a lot! He wanted God to destroy the city, not save it.

Leaving Nineveh, Jonah climbed a nearby hill. He wanted to watch what happened to the city—and pout. The sun was so hot that Jonah put branches over his head for shade. Then God had an idea. He made a thick vine with big leaves grow up quickly to keep Jonah cool. Jonah was very happy with the vine.

The next day God sent a worm to chew the vine so that it died. The hot sun and wind made Jonah weak. "I'd rather die than live!" he complained again. Now Jonah was even angrier than he had been before.

"Jonah, do you have any right to be angry?" God asked. "You have been concerned about this vine. But you did not take care of it. You did not make it grow. . . . Nineveh has more than 120,000 people. They can't tell right from wrong. . . . So shouldn't I show concern for that great city?"

Jonah had no answer. God had been very patient with him. Now Jonah finally understood. God loves *everyone* and wants them to know Him—even people that we don't like.

Questions:

1. What do you think it was like in the belly of a big fish?
2. Have you ever talked to someone about God who didn't know Him? What did you do?

Prayer:

Thank God for loving everyone. Ask for courage to tell others about Him—even people you don't like.

Deaf Israel Loses Fight

(2 Kings 13–17; Hosea 8:14; 12:7–10; 13:7–9; 14:4–9; Amos 2:6–16; 3:13–14; 5:11–15; 8:4–8)

For over a thousand years, God had worked many miracles for His people and gave them victory over their enemies. But the people preferred sin and false gods and did not obey God. They broke His heart.

God's prophets warned them, "Turn back to God, or your enemies will defeat you." But did they listen? No. So their kings grew weak and failed to lead them the right way. And their enemies grew stronger...and stronger.

King Ahab and his family were evil and served false gods. So when King Ahab went to battle, guess who won? Israel's enemies! They captured many cities and towns, the land God had promised Abraham.

Then Jehu became king. He did as God said. For a while. But he made the same mistake: He stopped obeying God. And Israel lost more land! Jehu's son King Jehoahaz had only 50 horsemen, ten chariots, and 10,000 soldiers left in his army. Then Jehoahaz listened to God's prophet Elisha. He asked God for help and God stopped the wars.

But the peace was short because Jehoahaz made a big mistake. He stopped following God. His son Jehoash disobeyed God too. And can you guess what happened? Right. Their enemies defeated them. God still loved the people and wanted to bless them. If only they could learn their lesson!

One day, King Jehoash went to see God's prophet, Elisha. Elisha promised him that Israel would defeat their enemies three times. And that's what happened! God blessed Israel whenever they turned back to Him even a little. Maybe they would learn.

Later, when Israel grew rich, they decorated their homes with ivory. They built high walls around their cities. They planted crops and had lots of food. Did they thank God for their wealth and obey Him? No! They kept serving false gods. They became proud. They cheated and robbed. The rich were mean to the poor, stealing their land and selling them as slaves! God hurt inside. Sin was destroying His people. So He sent his prophet Amos. "What you're doing is wrong!" he said.

"God says He'll crush you. Your warriors will run away in battle. God will tear down your fancy houses and you won't get to eat your crops. Hate evil! Love good! Be fair to one another! Then maybe God Almighty will have mercy on you."

Guess what? The people didn't listen. Still God waited patiently. Jeroboam II became king, then six more kings after him. But they didn't listen either. Finally, God had enough. He sent His prophet Hosea to say, "God will send fire on your cities. He sent you prophets. You didn't listen. So He'll attack you like a roaring lion. You're destroyed because you're against God your helper."

God helped Israel's cruel neighbor Assyria grow powerful. They built a huge army and took more and more of Israel's land. Finally, the king of Assyria tore down Israel's fortresses and fancy houses. The Assyrians destroyed Israel so badly that it never became a nation again!

But God still loved His people. Hosea promised, "One day God will stop you from walking away from Him. He'll love you and turn His anger away from you. He'll make you strong and beautiful again. He'll answer your prayers and care for you. The wise person understands God's ways. The righteous follow them. But those who refuse to obey will fall." Do you think they listened?

Questions:

1. What would have happened if Israel listened to the prophets? Why?
2. When your parents or others correct you or warn you what will happen if you do wrong, how do you respond?

Prayer:

Ask for help to listen to correction and then to change. Thank God for wanting you to know and do right so that you can have a good life.

Isaiah, Prophet to Judah

(Isaiah 1:17–20; 2:22; 3:10; 5:13, 20–23; 6:1–13; 7:14; 9:2; 11:1–3; 29:13; 30:15; 37:7–9, 33–38; 42:1–3; 44:28; 49:15; 52:14; 53; 58:7–8)

Meanwhile in the kingdom of Judah, Isaiah entered the courtyard of Solomon's temple in the city of Jerusalem. Passing through the bronze pillars and stone doorway, he was barely inside when he saw a brilliant light. *What's happening?* Isaiah wondered, terrified. Then he saw God appearing on a great throne! Six-winged angels flew above Him crying, "Holy, holy, holy is the LORD who rules over all. The whole earth is full of His glory!" The stone doorway shook from their voices and smoke filled the temple.

Isaiah fell to his knees before the throne. He knew he wasn't pure enough to stand in God's presence! But an angel came to him and touched his lips to make them pure.

Then the LORD asked, "Who will I send?"

"Here I am," Isaiah answered, his heart thumping. "Send me!" Everything inside him wanted to serve God for the rest of his life! God was pleased with Isaiah's answer.

"Go and speak to these people," God said. But God knew they wouldn't listen.

Isaiah became a man with one mission: God spoke through Isaiah to the people and kings of Judah *for 60 years*. But, just as God had said, the people didn't listen. They said they loved God, but their hearts were far away from Him. Isaiah could see this by the unkind ways they treated one another.

"Learn to do what's right!" Isaiah urged. "Treat people fairly. Give hope to those who are beaten down."

God promised through Isaiah that "Even though your sins are bright red, they'll be as white as snow. . .If you're willing to change and obey Me, you'll eat the best food that grows on the land."

And God used Isaiah to warn the people: "You must follow me. You must obey me. If you do not, you will be killed with swords."

"Do right," Isaiah begged them, "and things will go well for you. You'll find peace, rest, and strength when you trust God." But the people didn't trust God.

One day Isaiah looked out his window to see Judah's

enemies surrounding the city wall of Jerusalem. *Knock! Knock!* Hezekiah, the king of Judah, sent his messengers to Isaiah's door. "Ask God to help us," they begged, "or we'll be crushed!" Unlike almost all the other kings of Judah, King Hezekiah loved and trusted God, as King David had.

"Don't worry," Isaiah said. "God told me, '[the king of Assyria] will not enter this city. He will not even shoot an arrow at it.'" The next morning, when the people of Jerusalem got up they found the enemy soldiers dead on the ground outside the city walls. God's angel had destroyed the Assyrian army at night with a plague. Because King Hezekiah trusted God, Judah was safe—for now.

But it broke Isaiah's heart when the people of Judah still refused to listen to his many warnings and turn back to God. He knew that one day they'd be taken captive to Babylon. But God promised through Isaiah that some of His people would return to Jerusalem some day. And King Cyrus would allow them to rebuild it.

Over and over, Isaiah saw God do what He said. The most amazing thing is that God showed Isaiah about Jesus! Isaiah told people about the coming Messiah. "The virgin is going to have a baby. She will give birth to a son. And He will be called Immanuel."

His voice cracked as he described what God showed him about the way the Messiah would suffer

for us. It was as if Isaiah was at the foot of the cross himself, a part of the crowd who crucified Jesus. "We looked down on Him," he said. "We didn't have any respect for Him. He suffered the things we should have suffered. He took on Himself the pain that should have been ours."

But through Jesus' suffering, God would bring about His plan to make things right again. This was the plan God had told Adam and Eve, Abraham, and David about long ago: Their descendant, the Messiah, would bless the whole world. Isaiah said this and wrote it down 700 years before Jesus was born!

Questions:

1. Imagine being Isaiah. What would it be like to know about the future?
2. If you served God for 60 years like Isaiah, how many of God's promises do you think you would see fulfilled?

Prayer:

Thank God for being faithful and keeping His promises. Ask for help to serve Him faithfully, even when it seems that others aren't.

The Weeping Prophet
(Jeremiah 1; 20–40; 52:17)

Many years later, Jeremiah, another prophet of God, stood watching people come and go in the temple courtyard. They were worshiping statues of false gods in *God's* house. *I'd like to shake them and make them see how wrong it is!* Jeremiah thought. When he could stand it no longer, he cried out God's warning, "You will be punished because you have sinned. You will be corrected for turning away from God. He is the LORD your God."

Priests ran from across the courtyard and grabbed him. They didn't like Jeremiah's message. It might upset the people in the temple and the priests wanted things

237

to stay just as they were. "You should die, Jeremiah!" they yelled, dragging him out of the temple. "Why do you prophesy these awful things?"

"With your own eyes you will see them die," he told the priests as they pushed him out the door. "God says He will hand all of the people of Judah over to the king of Babylonia."

"That does it!" the red-faced priests threatened. "We don't want to hear anything more from you. And don't *ever* come back!"

Jeremiah wasn't looking for a fight. He was just obeying God. When he was very young, God had said, "Before I formed you in your mother's body I chose you. Before you were born I set you apart to serve me. I appointed you to be a prophet to the nations."

"I don't know how to speak," Jeremiah had pleaded. "I'm only a child."

"Don't say 'I'm only a child,'" God had answered. "I am with you."

What could Jeremiah say then? He loved God, so he prophesied—and kept getting in trouble. But he had to speak! God's words were like a fire inside him!

Now Jeremiah couldn't go to the temple. But God was warning His people. They had to hear! So Jeremiah's assistant Baruch wrote down everything God gave Jeremiah to say. Baruch took his scroll to the temple and read it aloud.

When they heard Baruch, the people said, "The king

must hear this message." But King Jehoiakim didn't take God's word seriously. He even burned the scroll!

Finally, the Babylonian army came and took King Jehoiakim and some of the people captive to Babylon just as Jeremiah had warned. He told the new king, Zedekiah, "They'll be in Babylon 70 years before God brings them back. Then He'll restore our land and make it rich again. For now, it's important to obey the Babylonian king and live."

King Zedekiah didn't like his message either. From then on, Jeremiah suffered a lot for telling the truth. When the Babylonian army came back to surround Jerusalem, Jeremiah said, "Anyone who stays in the city will die. Surrender and you'll live."

The officials couldn't believe it. "Treason!" they cried. They threw Jeremiah into an empty well and left him to die. But God sent Ebed-Melech, a palace official, to pull him out. Soon Nebuzaradan, the Babylonian commander, broke down the city walls. He burned Jerusalem, destroyed God's temple, and carried away all the temple treasures. Even though Jeremiah had told the people this would happen, it broke his heart to see it. If only they'd listened and turned back to God!

Nebuzaradan found Jeremiah chained up with other captives. He said, "This happened because you people disobeyed your God. Come or stay, Jeremiah. You can choose."

The people who remained in Judah still needed God's word. So Jeremiah stayed with them. It was more important to him to serve God rather than choose an easier life in Babylon. God continued to speak through Jeremiah. God promised, "There'll come a time when I'll make a new covenant. I'll put my law in their minds and write it on their hearts. I'll be their God and they'll be My people." God still planned for the time when David's descendant would crush the serpent's head. Someday Satan would be defeated.

Questions:

1. How do you think Jeremiah felt when people threw him into the well for telling the truth?
2. Have you ever thought you were too young for something, like Jeremiah? What? What things could you do for God and others even though you're young?

Prayer:

Thank God that age doesn't matter to Him and that He can use you no matter how old you are. Ask for help to keep doing things His way, like Jeremiah.

Veggie Boys

(Daniel 1)

Fifteen-year-old Daniel and his friends followed other young captives like themselves through the huge gate into Babylon. They were all handsome, strong, intelligent, and able to learn new things quickly. Officials from King Nebuchadnezzar's court had picked them for "special training," whatever that meant.

Daniel pointed to rows of lions and bulls carved on the walls that lined the street. "Those must be Babylon's gods," he said quietly so the guards couldn't hear. "Following God will be even harder here. *Everyone* serves false gods." His three friends, Shadrach, Meshach, and Abednego nodded. They needed to be careful.

At last, the long line of captives climbed a flight of stairs and gathered in the palace courtyard. Now they would learn why they were here. Ashpenaz the chief official cleared his throat loudly. Pointing to a stone tablet covered in strange markings he announced, "You all must learn the Babylonian language and writings. After three years, King Nebuchadnezzar will test you and then choose some of you to serve him. While you're here, you'll eat food from the King's own table." Many of the young men grinned. The king's table had the best tasting food in the kingdom!

Ashpenaz signaled his servants to take the boys to their rooms. *Finally we can speak freely*, Daniel thought. "The king's food is not good," Daniel told his friends. "They don't follow the rules that God gave to Moses about what we should eat and how to cook it. And eating food from the king's table is just the first step. If we agreed to that, we might also be persuaded to do other things that displease God."

"But don't we have to do what the king says?" Shadrach asked.

Meshach shook his head. "Not if he tells us to disobey God."

"Exactly," Daniel nodded. "I've got an idea. Let's ask if we can eat only vegetables and water. That way we'll put God first."

Abednego frowned. "If we make a fuss, we may lose our chance to serve in the king's court."

"I know," Daniel shrugged. "But if we do things God's

way, He'll take care of us."

So they spoke with Ashpenaz. He liked the four Israelites but was afraid of Nebuchadnezzar. "The king has decided what you and your friends must eat and drink. If he sees you looking worse than the others, he'll kill me," he said.

So Daniel talked to the guard in charge of their group. "Please test us for ten days," he suggested. "Give us nothing but vegetables to eat. And give us only water to drink. Then compare us with the young men who eat the king's food. See how we look. After that, do what you want to."

The guard agreed. So for ten days the boys ate veggies—like onions, yams, carrots, potatoes, peas, barley, oats, and leeks. After ten days, the guard was amazed. The four Israelites looked healthier and better fed than those who'd eaten the king's rich food. "All right," he said. "You can have your plants and water."

Daniel grinned. "We've started out doing things God's way," he said. "He's already blessed us. Now they'll ask us to learn things that go against what God says. We have to *learn* it, but we don't have to *believe* it."

"Right!" Shadrach agreed. "We'll compare what they teach us to what God says. And we'll pray for help to know the truth and tell the difference between right and wrong."

So God helped them understand all kinds of things and gave them wisdom to know what was true. He helped them become all He wanted them to be. At the same time, they were able to please the king's officials.

Three years later, Ashpenaz called the four friends together and led them across a huge courtyard. It was the day of their big test. Today they would meet Nebuchadnezzar himself, the most powerful man in this part of the world.

As they approached his throne, Nebuchadnezzar's piercing black eyes examined them silently. Then the king began asking questions. At first the boys were nervous, but they got bolder as they realized they knew the answers. Nebuchadnezzar was impressed. These four boys were the best in the class. Yes, they were well suited to serve him!

From then on, Nebuchadnezzar often asked for their advice. Their answers were better than all the other wise men's because their wisdom came from God.

Questions:

1. Why do you think Daniel and friends looked healthier than the others?
2. Daniel and friends chose to do things God's way without compromising. God helped them do well. How can you follow their example?

Prayer:

Ask God for help in school and to recognize right from wrong.

The Fiery Furnace

(Daniel 3)

The three friends, Shadrach, Meshach, and Abednego, greeted one another eagerly. It had been months since they'd been together. "What's this all about?" Abednego asked, nodding at the huge crowd of men around them.

Meshach replied, "The king has called in all his leaders. He wants to unite the empire by making everyone worship the same god."

"Uh-oh," Shadrach said. "Does that mean the 90 foot golden statue I saw?"

"Yes," Meshach nodded. "And you can be sure our old 'friends' will be watching for any chance to get us in trouble." He pointed to some Babylonian leaders glaring at them across the courtyard.

"They're still jealous because we were promoted?" Abednego asked. "Well, there's no way we'll worship that statue. Our people disobeyed God for hundreds of years. Now it's time to be faithful to Him, no matter what."

"No matter what," the others agreed. "We'll trust God to take care of us."

A few days later, all the nobles strutted in their glittering robes and dazzling jewelry on the plain outside Babylon. The sun sparkled off rubies, emeralds, diamonds, and pearls. But the biggest attraction by far was the giant statue towering over them—Babylon's new "god."

A trumpet rang out. Everyone turned to the man standing beside the king's throne. "When you hear the music," he shouted, "you must fall down and worship the gold statue that King Nebuchadnezzar has set up. If you don't, you will be thrown into a blazing furnace right away." Shadrach, Meshach, and Abednego looked at one another. "No matter what," they whispered as one, and then prayed for God's strength.

The music began. Every man fell face down before the statue. Every man except Shadrach, Meshach, and Abednego! Their enemies peeked up at them from the ground, and grinned. Now they'd have their revenge.

King Nebuchadnezzar was furious when he heard. These three had publicly disobeyed him. "Is what I heard about you true?" he asked them angrily. "Don't you worship the gold statue I set up?" But even so, the king didn't want to lose good leaders. "I'll give you one more

chance," he bargained. "When the music starts again, if you worship the statue, well and good. But if you don't, you'll be thrown at once into a blazing furnace." He pointed to the tunnel covered in hard clay, which was used for making bricks. A fierce fire burned inside. "*Then* what god will be able to save you from my powerful hand?" Nebuchadnezzar scowled and stood up to frighten them.

Shadrach spoke respectfully. "We might be thrown into the blazing furnace. But the God we serve is able to bring us out of it alive. He will save us from your powerful hand. But," he added glancing at his friends, "we want you to know this. Even if we knew that our God wouldn't save us, we still wouldn't serve your gods."

Nearby, their enemies smirked. There'd be no saving these Jews now. The king bellowed, "Heat that furnace seven times hotter!"

Men threw more coal into the furnace and fanned the roaring flames higher. The captain signaled. Soldiers grabbed the three friends, tied them up, and carried them toward the furnace. The fire was so hot the soldiers staggered as they got near, tossed the friends through the doorway, and then collapsed, dead!

The king watched angrily. He'd show *them* for disobeying him! Suddenly he sat up in shock. "Didn't we tie *three* men up? Didn't we throw *three* men into the fire?" he asked, puzzled. "Look! I see four men walking around in the fire. They aren't tied up. And the fire hasn't even harmed them. The fourth man looks like a son of the gods." The jeering crowd fell silent. Surely the

king's eyes played tricks on him!

"You who serve the Most High God, come here!" the king shouted into the furnace, feeling a little foolish.

The three friends strolled out. There wasn't a mark on them! Their clothes were clean. Their hair was perfect. *Nothing* was burned. They didn't even smell of smoke!

Nebuchadnezzar stood open-mouthed. It wasn't possible—yet there they stood, unharmed. "May the God of these men be praised!" he cried in awe. "He saved them. They trusted in Him and were ready to die rather than worship any god except Him. No other god can save like this. From now on, anyone who speaks against their God will be punished." Then the king honored Abednego, Meshach, and Shadrach, and gave them another promotion.

God saved his faithful servants. Their miracle encouraged every captive Jew in Babylon that God would save His people when they were faithful to Him.

Questions:

1. What do you think it was like for the three being in the furnace with the LORD?
2. Name some times when it helps you to know God is with you.

Prayer:

Thank God for being with you all the time. Ask for help to remember He's especially close when you have troubles.

Enemies and Lions

(Daniel 6)

King Darius drummed his fingers impatiently on the arm of his throne. "Now what?" he muttered to himself. Two of the leaders over his entire kingdom and all the royal rulers had asked to see him. *Probably up to no good. I wish they could all be like Daniel,* he thought. Daniel had been serving Babylonian and now Persian kings for many years. In all that time, he'd never done anything wrong, could always be trusted, and he always did what he was supposed to. Daniel was such a good leader, Darius planned to put him in charge of the whole kingdom.

But the two leaders that worked with Daniel (and

all the rulers) didn't want to lose their power. That's why they asked to see the king. They couldn't find anything to blame on Daniel, but came up with another scheme to get him in trouble. "King Darius, may you live forever!" they greeted him, bowing before the throne.

"We've got an idea," they began. "We think you should make a special law. For the next 30 days, none of your people should pray to any god or man except to you. If they pray to anyone else, they should be thrown in the lion's den."

King Darius leaned back and stroked his chin. *Hmm, not a bad idea*, he thought. Like any king, he liked to display his power. Besides, it seemed harmless. "Okay, I'll do it," he told the group. But he wasn't thinking about Daniel, even though Daniel always said his wisdom and character came from God.

"Write it down in the law book. Then no one can change the order," the rulers urged. So the king did as they asked. Once he wrote it, it couldn't be changed—even by him.

Now Daniel heard that the king had signed the order, but he did what he had always done before. He went home to his upstairs room with its windows facing Jerusalem and prayed to God, three times a day. Talking to God was more important to Daniel than life! Of course, the royal rulers were just waiting to catch him and they ran to tell King Darius.

"The order must be obeyed. It can't be changed," Darius said, shaking his head sadly. "Not even for Daniel." He ordered his guards to arrest Daniel and went himself to watch as they threw Daniel into the lion's den, closing the opening with a huge stone. Darius sealed it his ring. Daniel was face to face with vicious, hungry lions and Darius could do nothing to help him now. He called to Daniel, "You always serve your God faithfully. So may He save you!" Then he returned to his palace.

King Darius was very troubled that night. Daniel had seemed so calm, but no one had *ever* survived a night in a lions' den. They kept the lions *very* hungry! Could Daniel's God really save him? Darius couldn't eat or sleep. He kept seeing Daniel's calm, hurt look. Finally, a faint pink lined the horizon. The sun was rising! He threw on some clothes and hurried down the echoing palace halls in the early morning chill, expecting the worst. Finally, he reached the lion's den.

"Daniel!" Darius called, "You serve the living God. You always serve him faithfully. So has He been able to save you from the lions?" He held his breath.

"Yes."

The king let out a cry of joy! He ordered the stone removed and Daniel lifted out. There was not a mark on him.

"My God sent His angel. And His angel shut the mouths of the lions," Daniel explained. "They haven't hurt me at all. That's because I haven't done anything

wrong in God's sight. I've never done anything wrong to you either, my king."

King Darius punished Daniel's enemies, and made a new law that everyone in his kingdom must honor and respect Daniel's God. He said, "He is the living God. He will live forever. His kingdom will not be destroyed. His rule will never end."

Daniel served the kings of Babylon and Persia for over seventy years, even though he was a captive. Then, just as Isaiah and Jeremiah said, King Cyrus let the Jews go home and rebuild Jerusalem.

Questions:

1. What do you think Daniel might have been thinking all night in the lions' den?
2. Daniel didn't let anything interfere with his talking to God regularly. What can you do to stop things getting in the way of your talking to God?

Prayer:

Ask God for help to get to know Him better and to spend time talking with Him regularly, like Daniel.

Nehemiah's Wall

(Ezra, Nehemiah)

Nehemiah shifted his weight in the saddle. It had been a long hard ride from Susa in Persia—over a thousand miles. But now the new governor of Judah stopped to view the city he had dreamed of seeing: Jerusalem! Many years before, the Babylonians had destroyed Jerusalem and taken its people captive. Now tired, broken down buildings sprawled untidily across a hill on the opposite side of the valley. Streets wove through dirty squares and piles of rubble. Mounds of broken stone lay scattered where a strong wall once stood. *It's far from the Jerusalem the exiles described,* Nehemiah thought sadly. *This is God's city, reduced to a garbage dump by sin. The whole world must laugh at us!*

Almost seventy years earlier King Cyrus had sent Zerubbabel and others to rebuild God's temple. Nehemiah strained to find it. There it was! *The only nice-looking building in the city*, he thought. Then Nehemiah spurred his horse into a canter and headed toward Jerusalem. Soon he'd worship God in His own city and rebuild the wall that protected it from its enemies!

Just then, Nehemiah noticed three riders nearby, Sanballat, Tobiah, and Gershom, who had come to check him out. He nodded coldly and rode past them. *I have a feeling those three are up to no good*, Nehemiah thought, as he headed down into the valley toward Jerusalem.

After he reached the city, Nehemiah called the Jewish leaders together. "God has heard our prayers," he said. "The king of Persia sent me to rebuild Jerusalem's walls and make it safe again. Everyone must help."

A few days later, cheerful voices shouted back and forth as the men began their work.

"Pitiful wall!" a voice sneered. Nehemiah looked up to see Sanballat the Horonite and Tobiah from Ammon. They were angry because they wanted the Jews and Jerusalem to stay weak. "If a fox climbed on your wall, it would topple!" Tobiah mocked. The workers turned red but kept working. Insults would not keep them from rebuilding the wall!

The word spread among neighboring nations: Jerusalem would soon have a new wall. It was already half done. Then new reports poured in. Robbers were attacking Jews in their fields and on the wall! "It's Tobiah and Gershom," Nehemiah was told. "They've stirred up

bandits to do this."

Nehemiah prayed for God's help. Then he brought all the Jews into Jerusalem for protection. He divided his workers into shifts. One shift worked while the other stood guard. Every man worked with one hand and carried a weapon in the other. If bandits appeared now, they were in for a fight! Slowly the workers cleared away rubble and fit rocks tightly together—and the wall rose higher.

Then one day, a messenger approached Nehemiah. He said, "Sanballat and Tobiah want to meet with you." Nehemiah was suspicious. If he went outside the city these men might hurt him. "No," he answered, "I'm too busy here."

A few days later, Sanballat's aide arrived with a scroll. "My master requests a meeting," he said. Nehemiah unrolled the scroll and read, "There's a rumor you're going to rebel and make yourself king of Judah. The king of Persia will hear about this. Let's talk."

Nehemiah glared at the aide. "This is nonsense and Sanballat knows it. So will the king. Send any report you want, I'm innocent. Now get out!" The man ran away. Threats didn't scare Nehemiah.

Sanballat and Tobiah were running out of ideas. They hired people to prophesy against Nehemiah or to trick and embarrass him. But Nehemiah prayed to God for strength and kept doing what God said.

Nehemiah and Ezra the priest gathered the people in the large square by the almost finished Water Gate. Ezra read God's Law to them from dawn to noon for seven

days. Leaders explained it so they would understand. When they heard God's Word, the people wept, because they were sorry for not obeying God. But Nehemiah said, "Stop crying. God's joy is your strength."

Then the people promised to follow God with all their hearts.

Not long after, the wall was finished! All the Jews gathered to celebrate. Along the top of the new wall, two choirs walked in opposite directions around the city singing praises to God. It almost seemed the stones themselves were singing!

God had helped the Jews overcome their enemies. They offered sacrifices of thanksgiving and shouted for joy. In fact, the noise of their celebration carried clear across the valley to where Sanballat, Tobiah, and Gershom sat. They kicked their horses crossly and galloped away.

Questions:

1. Nehemiah was discouraged many times. Name two times he might have been tempted to give up doing what was right.
2. Nehemiah and the Jews were unshakeable in doing what God wanted, and God blessed them. How can you be unshakeable in doing what God wants?

Prayer:

Ask God for help to continue following Him.

Queen's Courage

(Esther)

The young girl Hadassah peeked out the window of Mordecai's house in Susa. Soldiers dismounted from their horses and walked toward their door. "What do I do?" she whispered to her cousin Mordecai. At this time, the Jews were captives in Persia.

Mordecai hugged her gently. "Go with them. Xerxes, king of Persia, is looking for a new queen. They're taking beautiful young women like you to meet him. But," he laid a finger on her lips, "don't tell anyone you're a Jew. It's not safe. Use your Persian name, Esther."

Esther nodded and greeted the men who took her to Xerxes' palace. For a whole year, Esther got ready to meet the king. She wore silk robes and dazzling jewels. Her maids rubbed oils and perfumes into her skin to make it soft and smell wonderful.

Finally, it was Esther's night to go before the king. Xerxes loved Esther's gentle spirit and beauty right away. "This is my new queen," he said, placing the crown on her head. Still Esther told no one she was a Jew. Not even the king.

Mordecai walked near the towering palace gates every day and checked to see that Esther was all right. One day, an important official named Haman passed through the gates where Mordecai worked. Everyone bowed to Haman, except Mordecai. Haman was furious! "I'll show Mordecai and all the Jews what happens when they refuse me!" he fumed. "I'll trick King Xerxes into passing a law to destroy them!"

Haman's evil plan worked. The king's order went throughout the empire: On the 13th day of the 12th month, every Jew in the empire must be destroyed— young and old, even women and children.

When Mordecai heard, he tore his clothes, covered himself with ashes, and sobbed loudly in deep sorrow. *Maybe Esther can do something,* he hoped. So he sent her a message: "Beg the king's mercy for our people."

"But there's a law," Esther wrote back. "If anyone enters the king's court without an invitation, the king must raise his gold rod or they'll be killed—even me!"

"You live in the king's palace. But don't think that just because you are there you will be the only Jew who will escape," warned Mordecai. "What if you don't say anything at this time? Then help for the Jews will come

from another place. But you and your family will die. Who knows? It's possible that you became queen for a time just like this." Mordecai knew God had a plan for Esther's life—and for the Jews.

Esther closed her eyes and prayed for courage. "Have our people fast for me for three days," she wrote Mordecai. "Then I'll go to the king. If I have to die, I'll die."

Three days later Esther put on her royal robes and jewels. Trembling slightly, she entered the king's court and stood quietly. *Will he be happy I came or send me to prison?* She wondered. Then Xerxes raised his rod to her! "What is it, Queen Esther? I'll give you whatever you ask," he said warmly.

Esther approached the king. "Oh king," she said, "please come to a banquet tomorrow and I'll tell you what I want. And bring Haman."

Haman puffed up with pride at the invitation! He bragged to his wife and friends about how important he was—and how he hated Mordecai and the Jews! *Soon*, he gloated, *I'll have my revenge.*

Esther's banquet was a great success. Finally, King Xerxes again asked, "What can I do for you? Anything you want!"

"I hope you will be pleased to let me live. That's what I want," Esther blurted. "Please spare my people. That's my appeal to you. My people and I have been sold to be destroyed."

The king's jaw dropped. "Who'd dare do such a thing?" he demanded, jumping to his feet. Remember,

even King Xerxes didn't know Esther was a Jew.

Esther pointed. "Haman!"

"Take this man and punish him!" the king ordered.

"Please stop Haman's plan too," Esther begged.

Xerxes hung his head. "Even I can't change the law."

"Then make another law," she suggested. "Let the Jews defend themselves from their enemies." The king agreed. So the Jews got together in their cities and attacked those who were trying to destroy them. No one could stand up against them and they were saved! Then the king gave Mordecai Haman's old job.

Esther was in the right place at the right time to help God's plan move forward. In time, the Jews returned to their own land to get ready for the One who would make all things right.

Questions:

1. What made Esther decide to risk her life to save the Jews?

2. If you had been Esther, would you have had the courage to do what was right? Why or why not?

Prayer:

Ask God to help you be ready and willing to be part of His plan by always choosing to do what's right.

272

Time for God's Promise

(Matthew 1:18–25; Luke 1:26–56; John 1:1–18)

Mary carried grain onto the flat roof of her family's house in Nazareth and spread the grain out to dry. The young girl smiled to herself. *Thump! Thump! Scrape!* Joseph was at work in his carpentry shop down the street. She climbed down from the roof and paused in the shade at the bottom, hugging herself. She was so lucky to be engaged to the most wonderful man in the village. In Galilee! In the whole Roman Empire!

Four hundred years had passed since God had brought His people back from captivity in Babylon. Now they were serving God and keeping His Laws. God had worked so many years to get them ready. Mary knew about God's promise that one of David's descendants would crush Satan's head—and bless the whole world. *Will He come in my lifetime?* Mary wondered, as she daydreamed about her upcoming marriage to Joseph.

"Greetings, Mary." Mary whirled to face a tall man in blinding white clothes standing in the tiny courtyard. "The LORD has given you special favor. He is with you," he continued.

Mary trembled. His voice was so powerful! *He must be an angel*, she thought. *But why did he say that about me? I don't deserve special favor from God.*

The angel said, "Do not be afraid, Mary. God is very pleased with you. You will become pregnant and give birth to a son. You must name him Jesus. He will be great and will be called the Son of the Most High God. The Lord God will make Him a king like His father David of long ago. He will rule forever over His people, who came from Jacob's family. His kingdom will never end."

Mary touched the wall, shaking. The angel was talking about the Messiah—the promised One God would send to make things right with Himself again! *She* would give birth to the *Messiah?* "How can this happen?" she asked. "I'm not married yet."

"The Holy Spirit will come to you. The power of the Most High God will cover you. So the holy one

born will be called the Son of God. . . . Nothing is impossible for God."

"I serve the LORD," Mary whispered. "May it happen to me just as you said it would." The angel vanished and Mary crumpled to the ground. Had that just happened? Yes! After a while, she wandered into the house in a daze. *What will Joseph say?* she wondered. Part of her wanted to run and tell him. Would he believe her? *Better leave it to God. Joseph has to be part of this. I'll need lots of help to raise God's Son.*

Four months later, when people could see Mary was pregnant, the talk started. Mary told her family the truth and they tried to believe her, but her story of an angel seemed far-fetched.

When Joseph heard the gossip, he felt as if it would rip out his heart. *How could Mary do this?* He sat with his head in his hands, rocking back and forth in grief. *I love her anyway. I'll make things as easy as I can for her. I'll. . .I'll send her away. Quietly.* He went to the village synagogue where they studied God's Word and cried out to God.

That night Joseph tossed and turned. When he finally fell asleep, an angel appeared to him in a dream. "Joseph, son of David," the angel said, "don't be afraid to take Mary home as your wife. The baby inside her is from the Holy Spirit. She is going to have a Son. You must give Him the name Jesus. That is because He will save His people from their sins."

Joseph woke up joyful. Mary hadn't sinned. She was favored by God! Isaiah's prophecy had said, "The virgin is going to have a son."

Mary heard Joseph's voice outside and cringed. Had he finally come to break off their engagement? "Mary, come here," her father called. Mary timidly entered the room, eyes on the floor. She couldn't stand it if Joseph hated her. "Joseph has come to make you his wife."

Mary looked up quickly. Joseph beamed. "An angel told me the truth in a dream," he said, putting his arms around Mary. "The baby's name will be Jesus!"

Questions:

1. What would it be like to have an angel visit you?
2. Mary and Joseph agreed to be God's partners in His plan. How would you respond to being God's partner in something He wanted to do? What if it would be embarrassing or scary?

Prayer:

Thank God for bringing His plan to pass in the world and in your life. Tell God if He wants you to be His partner, you will.

Born in a Barn?

(Luke 2:1–7)

Joseph burst into the house shedding dust and stone shavings. Mary looked up from weaving cloth for the baby's birth. *Almost finished*, she thought.

"Remember how we've tried to figure out the prophecies about the Messiah?" Joseph asked. Mary nodded. "Well, the Roman Emperor has called a census! Everyone has to go to their family town to be counted."

Mary's face lit up. "That's Bethlehem for us because you're from King David's line!" she exclaimed. "So that's how Micah's prophecy will come true." Mary laughed. "I wondered how God's Son could be born in Bethlehem when we live in Nazareth."

"Exactly! But the baby's due any day and it's almost 70 miles to Bethlehem," Joseph said, worried. He paced around their small house, avoiding the table he'd made for her.

"God will take care of us, Joseph," Mary said, catching his hand.

"Well, if we have to go, the sooner the better. We could be gone months if I know the Romans. They check everything at least four times. I'll take my tools."

Two mornings later, in the light of a flickering torch, Mary climbed onto the donkey they'd named Micah and settled among their few bags of provisions. Joseph fussed, making sure she was comfortable, then led Micah slowly off. Mary gazed one last time at the tiny house where they'd been so happy.

As dawn streaked the eastern sky with pink, the couple reached the main road. Mary dismounted and stretched. Soon, they heard other travelers approaching. Joseph called a greeting and helped Mary remount. They all traveled together toward Jerusalem with others joining them along the way. It seemed as though everyone in Israel was on the road because of the census.

Exhausted, Mary said good-bye to the last of their group in Jerusalem. *Only six more miles*, she told herself, watching the sheep play on the rocky fields beside the road. Shepherds and their dogs lounged nearby in the shade of stunted trees.

They heard the noise long before they reached

Bethlehem, nestled against the side of a hill. People and animals crowded the narrow streets, talking and laughing. Merchants sold their wares and everyone bustled about. Mary looked at Joseph in dismay.

"It will be okay," Joseph said, patting her hand. Pushing through the crowds, Joseph found a spot next to a pillar. He helped Mary down, and tethered Micah beside her. "Just sit here and rest," he said. "I'll find us a room." Mary nodded. All she wanted was a quiet place to lie down.

Joseph went in search of the inn. When he found it, it too was bursting at the seams. "No room," he was told. He looked for other places. Some people had opened their homes to make a few extra coins. But they were all more than full.

"Dear God," Joseph prayed. "Mary's exhausted. You brought us here to fulfill Your Word. Please help us find a safe place for Mary to have Your Son."

He tried one more place. A man and a woman opened the door. "My wife is about to have our first son," Joseph said. "Please help."

The man and his wife talked quietly to one another. Then the man turned back to Joseph. "All I have," he said, "is a corner of my stable. But it's warm and dry." He led Joseph around the house, into a small cave. Several donkeys and sheep munched food in a manger, ignoring the humans. The far corner of the stable was empty.

Straw will make a soft bed, water's nearby, and it's

quiet, Joseph thought. *Thank you, God.*

"We'll take it," he told the innkeeper. Then he went to get Mary and Micah and settle them in. Mary sighed as she stretched out on the soft straw. *At last*, she thought, *we're ready.*

A few nights later it was time. Joseph ran for the innkeeper's wife and helped as much as he could. Soon a baby cried! Joseph rushed to Mary's side. A tiny baby boy lay in her arms—the baby promised from the beginning. "God's Son," Joseph whispered. "Born in a stable. No one expected that. Thank You, God, for keeping us safe." Mary wrapped the baby in the cloth she'd woven and laid Him tenderly in the straw-filled manger.

Questions:
1. Do you know the story of how you were born? Ask your parents to tell you about it.
2. What does it mean to you that God sent His Son Jesus? How do you think Mary felt?

Prayer:
Thank God for sending His Son Jesus and for giving you a family.

Unusual Witnesses

(Luke 2:8–20)

Young Zebediah pulled his camel hair coat tight and stepped over the ewe and her lamb. He fingered his slingshot, glancing around to make sure all was quiet. Bright moonlight picked out the pale sheep scattered over the hillside near Bethlehem. But what was *that?* Zeb had never seen that star before! *A new star? Is that possible?* he wondered, as he walked back to join the other shepherds around the fire.

"There's a new star," Zeb said, sitting down. They stared at him. What could he be talking about? But before they could say anything more, a golden light flashed and awe washed over them.

"Do not be afraid," a deep, comforting voice said. Their fear vanished. "I bring you good news of great joy. It is for all the people. Today in the town of David a Savior has been born to you. He is Christ the LORD." The shepherds looked at one another, astonished. The Messiah? A *baby? Here?*

"Here is how you'll know I'm telling you the truth," the angel continued. "You will find a baby wrapped in strips of cloth," he paused, "and lying in a manger."

Suddenly the whole sky burst into song with choirs of angels praising God. The music poured through Zeb as if his whole body knew the song and wanted to join in. Tears filled his eyes. "May glory be given to God in the highest heaven!" the angels sang, "And may peace be given to those He is pleased with on earth!" Then they rose into heaven, still singing.

After a time Zeb whispered, "Why did God tell us? We're the last people anyone would tell."

"God must want everyone to know!" one suggested. "Let's go to Bethlehem. I want to see this amazing thing for myself!" They grabbed their staffs and hurried into town, leaving their sheep.

How will we find Him with so many people here? Zeb wondered. They threaded their way through travelers sleeping in the streets. "A manger means a stable," he said to the other shepherds. "Let's split up and check out all the stables in town. Whoever finds Him, whistle." That was their signal for a lost sheep who had been found!

It was a good plan. Two started on the west. One on the east. Others went from north to south. Zeb and his partner moved quickly through the dark streets, past the sounds of voices and laughter muted by shutters and doors. They peeked into stables at snoring animals and people sleeping in straw by donkeys or goats. But no baby in a manger.

Suddenly a whistle pierced the quiet. The two shepherds ran toward it through narrow streets, leaping over sleeping bodies. The rap, rap of their sandals echoed off the walls, waking people as they passed. They broke out of an alleyway and then stopped. There were their friends crowding around a small cave behind a house. Suddenly nervous, the two joined them. What—who— would they find?

A young woman sat with one hand draped over a tiny newborn she'd laid to sleep in a manger. Her eyes widened. A strong man stepped behind her, questioning them with his eyes.

The shepherds dropped to their knees in the straw. Zeb couldn't take his eyes off the baby. *The Savior*, he thought with awe. *The Messiah. Just as the angel said. Oh wow, oh wow, oh wow!*

"Who are you?" the man asked finally.

The shepherds began telling Mary and Joseph about the angel, then the choirs, then the music! "It seemed all heaven was celebrating," Zeb exclaimed, as each shepherd added details to the wondrous story. He studied the

couple as they tried to take in everything the shepherds said. Their eyes were wide with wonder and Mary's face glowed a soft pink. After a time, Joseph thanked the shepherds for coming. Now it was time for Mary and the tiny Messiah to sleep.

But the shepherds never slept that night. They told everyone they knew: "The Messiah's here! And we've seen Him." Why did God bring lowly shepherds to see His newborn Son? Because He knew they'd believe the angels, and share His joy! God wanted everyone to know.

Questions:

1. What would it have been like to be one of the angels sent to the shepherds?
2. Who can you tell about Jesus?

Prayer:

Ask for opportunities to tell other people that God sent His Son Jesus into the world because He loves us.

The Magi
and the King

(Matthew 2:1–23)

The wise men looked at home in the torch-lit, gold-decorated marble hall. Their gold-embroidered silk robes glittered with jewels and their soft slippers whispered across the inlaid floor. A guard beckoned, "King Herod will see you now."

The magi approached the scowling, bulky man on the throne. "Greetings," one said respectfully. "Where is the child who has been born to be king of the Jews?"

Herod clenched his jaw and tried to hide his growing irritation. "Sadly, there's no such child here."

"But when we were in the east, we saw His star. Now we have come to worship Him," another wise man explained. "If not here, where?"

"I asked the chief priests and teachers of the law this very question." Herod said impatiently, waving a hand.

A small man in a scribe's simple white robes stepped into the light and cleared his throat. "Our scriptures say the Christ is to be born in Bethlehem. Micah prophesied this about the ruler who would come to shepherd Israel."

"When did this star appear?" Herod quizzed the wise men.

"Almost two years ago, now," they answered. "Our travels were long."

Herod's eyes narrowed as he considered this news. His crooked smile gave the wise men shivers. He told them, "Go! Make a careful search for the child. As soon as you find him, bring me a report. Then I can go and worship him too."

Back among their own servants, the wise men agreed: Herod was one dangerous man! But the important thing now was to get to Bethlehem. As they mounted their camels and left the lights of Jerusalem behind, the star they had followed for so long shone brightly above them.

Finally, they were there. Bethlehem! But Bethlehem had many people. How would they know where to find the child? Then they noticed. The star had stopped above a small house on the west side of town. The magi shouted in joy. There could be no question. God was still leading them! But what a strange place for a king.

The next day, the magi knocked on the weathered

door of the poor house. They held their breath as footsteps approached and a strong man with tousled hair opened the door. "Is there a child here?" one asked him with a slight bow. "We seek the King of the Jews."

The man nodded with a slight smile, stepped back, and invited them in. They crowded into a simply furnished room. "Mary," the man called, "Jesus has visitors."

A bouncy two-year-old with dark eyes and curly hair pushed aside a woven door and smiled. The magi fell to their knees in worship, faces on the mud floor. Yes! This was the One they searched for. They recognized God's special favor even on one so small.

"We brought gifts to honor You," one wise man told Jesus, offering a box full of gold. "Thank you," Jesus said and promptly sat down to explore the coins.

A small box came next: Frankincense—a perfume fit for God. Its sweet smell filled the room. Myrrh was last. Jesus looked up to search his parents' faces. Was it okay to accept these expensive gifts? *Yes,* their eyes said, *yes, they belong to you.*

The wise men told Joseph and Mary about their journey and what God had said. Then they left the small family, hearts full of wonder. That night God warned them, "Don't return to Herod. Go home a different way." So when they left the next day, they avoided Jerusalem.

Meanwhile, Herod waited for the magi's report. But it wasn't so he could go to worship this supposed "king of the Jews." Herod wanted to stop Him before He became

a threat! When the magi didn't return, Herod flew into a rage. "Send soldiers to Bethlehem!" he screamed. "Kill all boys two years old and under!"

But an angel warned Joseph in a dream. "Get up!" he said. "Take the child and His mother and escape to Egypt. Stay there until I tell you to come back. Herod is going to search for the child. He wants to kill Him." Joseph quickly woke Mary, packed their few possessions, loaded up their donkey, Micah, and wrapped Jesus in a blanket. Quietly, he led the little donkey along deserted streets and out of town. They hurried south all night then joined a caravan headed for Egypt. And they made it out safe.

Questions:

1. What's your favorite part of this story?
2. God didn't tell only shepherds. He told people in other countries too because Jesus came for everyone. Talk about ways you can help people in other countries know about Jesus.

Prayer:

Thank God that Jesus came for everyone. Ask Him to help people everywhere know Him. Pray for any missionaries you know.

The Boy at the Temple

(Luke 2:41–51)

J oseph, Mary, and Jesus stood on the Mount of Olives
overlooking Jerusalem. Thousands of people poured into
the city for Passover. Jesus' eyes shone as he pointed to
the white and gold temple below them—Herod's temple.
"Look, Dad. The temple's already full of people."

From a distance, the huge Court of Gentiles looked
like an upended anthill with colorful, noisy ants rushing
in every direction. Baaing, bleating, and cooing animals
added to the din.

Jesus was 12 years old now. He was learning how
important the temple was in the life of the Jews. *Our
ancestors have worshipped God in the Jerusalem temple for*

hundreds of years, he thought. "Tell me again about bringing me to the temple when I was a baby," he pleaded, as they headed down into the city.

"Well," Joseph began, "you were only a couple months old when your mother and I took you to the temple in Jerusalem. The Law of the LORD says, 'The first boy born in every family must be set apart for the LORD.'"

"And shortly after we arrived," Mary chimed, "an old man named Simeon came over to us. He said that God promised him that he would see the Messiah before he died. So every day he waited in the temple to see the Messiah. When we walked in, God's Spirit told Simeon, 'This is the One.'"

Jesus was quiet for a long time thinking about what that could mean. Then he saw some of his friends just ahead. "Hey, Jesus," they called. "Come walk with us."

"Is that okay, Dad?" Jesus asked.

"Go ahead," Joseph replied. "We'll catch up with you later." Jesus ran off. He was always careful to respect and obey his parents. That's why Mary and Joseph became so worried later on.

After the Feast, the crowds quickly disappeared as everyone headed toward home. Mary and Joseph began the long trek back to Nazareth. "Have you seen Jesus?" Mary asked.

"Not recently," Joseph answered. "He's probably with his friends." They were part of a huge crowd traveling in the same direction. So they continued walking all day

until they stopped for the night.

"Have you seen Jesus?" Mary asked their relatives.

"Have you seen Jesus?" Joseph asked the men setting up tents.

Everywhere they went the answer was the same. "No."

Mary panicked. "Oh, Joseph. What if we've lost Him?"

Joseph took Mary's hands in his and comforted her. "God has seen us through many things, Mary. He knows where Jesus is. Let's head back to Jerusalem and look for him there." For three days, they looked everywhere they thought a 12-year-old boy might be. Yet no Jesus. They began to lose hope and Mary was sick with grief.

"Oh, God! Joseph cried in prayer. "We've run out of ideas. Please show us where Jesus is!"

"There's one place we haven't looked," Mary brightened. "Let's go to the temple."

They entered the Court of Gentiles that had been so crowded the week before. Today it was almost empty. Then they noticed some people gathered at the far end of Solomon's Porch. Frantic, they walked over. Half a dozen of the most respected teachers in Jerusalem sat before students and visiting teachers. Then Mary heard a familiar-sounding young voice ask a question. She looked at Joseph. *Could it be?* they wondered.

Silence followed the child's question. Finally, a rabbi asked *him* a question. The young voice answered the tough question correctly, as sounds of amazement rose from the small crowd around them. Jesus was teaching!

Then Jesus saw His parents. He smiled, got up, and went right to them.

"Son," Mary asked sternly, "why have you treated us like this? Your father and I have been worried about you. We have been looking for you everywhere."

Jesus looked from Mary to Joseph, puzzled. "Why were you looking for Me?" he asked. "Didn't you know I had to be in My Father's house?" But Mary and Joseph didn't understand what he meant. "I've been learning so much!" Jesus said, his eyes shining.

"Well, let's go home now," Joseph said quietly. The three moved toward the gate, with Jesus talking the whole way.

Jesus went back to Nazareth with his parents. He grew wise, strong, and more and more pleasing to God and to people. And His mother kept all these memories like a secret treasure in her heart, even when she didn't completely understand.

Questions:

1. What do you think it would have been like to see Herod's Temple during Passover?
2. What are some of the ways you can learn more about God?

Prayer:

Ask for help to obey God and your parents—and ask God to remind you if you forget what they've said.

John, Jesus, and the Jordan

(Matthew 3:1–17; Mark 1:1–12; Luke 3:1–23; John 1:19–34)

Repent and turn away from your sins!" the barefoot man in the rough camel hair shirt cried. A crowd of people lined the riverbank, huddled in the shade of the tamarisk trees. They had come from all over Judah to hear John, called "the Baptist." Some were there only because they were curious. But others really wanted to hear what John had to say.

John adjusted his leather belt and waded into the waters of the Jordan River. Soon he would invite others to join him in the river to be baptized. *I know You want them to be ready for the Messiah,* Lord, John prayed silently. *Give me the right words to say so I can help them.*

"Who are you? Are you Elijah?" someone from the crowd shouted. John was used to the question. People asked him all the time. He answered carefully.

"I am not."

"Are you the Prophet we've been expecting?" another voice prodded him.

"I'm the messenger who is calling out in the desert, 'Make the way for the Lord straight.'"

"If you are not the Christ, why are you baptizing people?" a Pharisee asked, trying to trick John. John loved this question because it gave him a chance to tell people about the One who was coming.

"I baptize people with water," John answered, his voice ringing across the river. "But One is standing among you whom you do not know. He is the One who comes after me. I am not good enough to untie his sandals." John was speaking about the Messiah.

People were really listening now, so John went on. He told them it wasn't good enough just to be one of Abraham's descendants. They needed to show they were ready for the Messiah by a changed heart.

"What should we do then?" someone cried.

"If you have extra clothes, share with those who don't. You tax collectors, don't collect more than you should. And you," he pointed to Roman soldiers in leather armor listening closely, "don't charge people wrongly or force them to give you money. Be satisfied with your pay."

John's preaching made people think about their own lives. "I want to be ready for Messiah!" a man cried suddenly, stepping into the water. Others took up the call and a crowd waded into the Jordan's muddy waters to be baptized. This would show their desire to obey God and their belief that the promised Messiah was coming soon.

When the crowd had dwindled until only a few were left, including John's disciples or followers, a Man stepped out from the shadow of tamarisk trees. Petals from their white and pink flowers fell on His shoulders as He walked forward and stepped into the waters.

John stopped in surprise. He hadn't seen this Man for years, but it was his cousin Jesus. Something about Jesus made John feel that he needed to repent.

"Baptize me, John," Jesus said. He knew it was time to begin the special work His Father God had sent Him to do. Baptism was a sign that He was obedient to God and ready to do all God wanted.

"No," John replied humbly. "I need to be baptized by you. So why do You come to me?"

"Let it be this way for now," Jesus answered gently. "It's right for us to do this. It carries out God's holy plan."

John prayed, took a deep breath, and did as Jesus asked. As Jesus came up out of the water praying, suddenly the heavens were opened. Jesus looked up and saw the Spirit of God coming down on Him like a dove.

Then God the Father spoke from heaven. To some

people His voice sounded like thunder. *How can this be?* they wondered. *The skies are cloudless!* But Jesus heard the words within the thunder. "This is My Son," God said, "and I love Him. I am very pleased with Him." Jesus' face shone as He walked out of the Jordan, passed beneath the trees, and disappeared over the bank toward the desert to pray.

Questions:

1. What would it have been like to suddenly see the dove and hear God's voice from heaven like thunder? What might you have seen and heard?
2. Jesus was God's Son before He was born as a child. What do you think it would have been like growing up as a human even though He was God?

Prayer:

Thank Jesus that even though He's God, He came to earth for you.

Rocky Road Rumble

(Matthew 4:1–11; Mark 1:12–13; Luke 4:1–13)

The sun was so hot that it made Jesus dizzy just to move. He staggered to a boulder and dropped into its shade. His body now was skinny and dark from the sun. He'd been fasting in this brown wilderness for 40 days with nothing to eat.

Jesus leaned wearily against the rock. God had brought Him to this desert right after John baptized Him. The whole 40 days He'd struggled and prayed. Jesus knew he must stay completely faithful to His Heavenly Father to do the work He had for Him on earth.

"Well, well, well," an oily voice said. "Look what we have here." It was Satan. He looked pleased with himself.

"You don't look so good," he mocked. "In fact, You look hungry. If You're the Son of God," his voice was doubtful, "prove it and tell these stones to become bread."

Jesus looked at the barren valley growing nothing but rocks and boulders. He was so hungry His stomach had given up rumbling! Jesus was God's Son, so He could turn the rocks into bread. But His Heavenly Father had asked Him to fast. Jesus wasn't going to put His own needs ahead of obeying God! He squinted red-rimmed eyes at Satan. "It is written, 'Man doesn't live only on bread. He also lives on every word that comes from the mouth of God.'"

Satan hid a flash of anger and forced a smile instead. "Come!" he beckoned Jesus. Suddenly they stood on the highest part of Herod's Temple looking down on the crowds and the Kidron valley, far, far below them. To the south, the sun sparkled off the Pool of Siloam. Jesus licked His lips. His whole body ached for water!

"If You are the Son of God," Satan tried to make Jesus doubt it, "throw Yourself down." He grinned slyly, "it is written, 'The LORD will command His angels to take care of you. They will lift you up in their hands. Then you won't trip over a stone.'"

Satan thought he was clever, quoting God's Word. He wanted Jesus to hurt himself. He knew what he asked was foolish. But Jesus loved and studied the Scriptures— He couldn't get enough of them!—so He knew Satan was using God's Word wrongly.

"It is also written, 'Do not put the LORD your God to the test,'" He said.

Satan frowned. Jesus wasn't falling for his lies. He'd have to offer Jesus the most tempting prize of all. So he took Jesus to a very high mountain. He showed Him all the sparkling kingdoms of the world. He waved his arm broadly, suggesting that everything on earth belonged to him and he could do whatever he wanted with it. Turning to Jesus like a salesman with a good deal, Satan said, "If You bow down and worship me, I will give You all of this."

Satan paused to let the power of his offer sink in. He wanted to convince Jesus that his lies made sense, just as he had with Adam and Eve in the garden. He seemed to offer Jesus the chance to make things right between God and mankind very easily.

Jesus' mission *would* be tough. But Satan didn't understand love. Jesus wanted God's kingdom for His Father and for us, not for Himself. Jesus knew that God is love and is the *only* One who deserves our worship. So He looked Satan right in the eye and said, "Get away from Me, Satan. Scripture says, 'Worship the Lord your God. Serve only Him.'"

Satan snarled, angrily gathered his robes around him, and left. Jesus leaned back against His rock, smiling. God had helped Him stay strong and do what was right.

Suddenly, a sound made Jesus turn. God had sent His angels to take care of Him. "Thank You, Father," He

whispered.

Questions:

1. The devil used lies to try to get Jesus to do wrong. What did Jesus use to protect Himself? Why?
2. Be like Jesus and memorize some Bible verses. Try this verse: "Children obey your parents. . .because it's the right thing to do" (Ephesians 6:1). When you're tempted to disobey, say it aloud to help you remember what's right and not give in to temptation.

Prayer:

Thank God for giving you His Word to protect you. Ask for help to learn and understand His truth in it.

Who Is This Miracle Man?

(Luke 5:1-11; John 2: 1-1 1;
Luke 7:11-17; Matthew 14:1-33;
Mark 6:34-52; Luke 9:10-17;
John 6:1-24; Matthew 8:27)

Simon was a fisherman. Every night he caught fish from the Sea of Galilee to sell at market the next day. Simon loved everything about fishing—the hard physical work, the sound of water lapping against the boat, the quiet nights at sea, even the smell of fish!

One morning, Simon was ready to go home when Jesus appeared with a big crowd following him. "Can I sit in your boat awhile to teach?" Jesus asked.

"Sure," Simon answered.

After Jesus finished speaking, He told Simon, "Go out into deep water. Let the nets down so you can catch some fish." Simon said he'd fished all night with no luck.

But he did what Jesus said. When he got to the middle of the lake, he let down the nets. When he pulled them in, they were so full of fish that they started to break. He called another boat to help him take in the fish! *This must be God's work*, Simon thought. When he got to shore, he fell on his knees.

"Don't be afraid," Jesus said. "And from now on you will catch people." Simon left his boat on shore and followed Jesus right away. Jesus changed his name to Peter (meaning "rock").

Soon Jesus had 12 disciples—men who would go wherever He went and learn from Him. They were: Simon Peter and his brother Andrew, James and John the sons of Zebedee, Philip, Bartholomew, Thomas, Matthew, James son of Alphaeus, Thaddaeus, Simon the Zealot and Judas Iscariot. At first, none of them knew who Jesus really was. But Jesus showed them by what He did.

Later, Jesus and His followers walked to the small town of Nain. *God must have something for Jesus to do here*, Peter thought. *But what's this? A funeral?* A weeping woman walked with slumped shoulders before the open coffin of her dead son. Many townspeople followed.

Jesus' face softened. "Don't cry," He told the grieving woman. Everyone stopped. "Young man, I say to you, get up!" Jesus commanded. Immediately, the dead man sat up and began talking! His mother cried in joy and people praised God saying, "A great prophet has appeared among us."

Soon crowds followed Jesus and His disciples everywhere. One day, Jesus went out in a boat to be alone. Thousands of people followed along the shore to where Jesus stopped to teach. When evening neared, Peter said, "Lord, there is nothing here. Send the people away to buy food."

"You give them something to eat," Jesus answered, looking at His disciples.

"We have only five loaves of bread and two fish," Andrew explained. About 5,000 were there!"

Jesus looked at the crowd. They seemed so lost and helpless. "Have them sit down in groups of fifty," He said.

Jesus thanked God and blessed the food, giving pieces to each disciple. *Maybe I can feed the first group*, Peter thought. But soon, *everyone* was full and they gathered 12 baskets of leftovers! Later, he told His disciples to get in the boat and go to Bethsaida ahead of him. Then He sent the crowd away and went into the hills to pray.

About three in the morning, Jesus returned to the shore. In the moonlight, He saw His disciples struggling against strong wind and waves far out on the lake. Jesus wanted to be with them, so He began walking toward them on the water.

John saw Him first and thought it was a ghost! The disciples were terrified and rowed with all their might.

"Don't be afraid," Jesus called.

Peter thought he recognized the voice. "Lord, is it

you? If it is, tell me to come to You on the water," he shouted.

"Come."

Peter swallowed, stepped out of the boat onto the water, and walked! But when he looked away from Jesus to the choppy waves, he started sinking. "Lord! Save me!" Peter screamed.

"Why did you doubt Me?" Jesus asked, catching him. Peter held on until they got into the boat. At once, the wind stopped and the moon drew its silver path across still water.

After all the disciples had seen, this impressed them most. "Even the wind and waves obey Him," they marveled. They began to understand that something was very different about this teacher.

Questions:

1. What do Jesus' miracles show you about God?
2. How would you feel if God did a big miracle in your life, something you needed?

Prayer:

Tell God that you'd like Him to show you His power and love in big and small ways.

People Matter Most

(Matthew 12:1–14; Mark 10:46–52; Mark 1:40–44; Luke 4:14–30; 13:10–17)

It was the Sabbath, the special Jewish day of rest, and people had gathered in the synagogue in Nazareth to pray and hear God's Word. Jesus was there, too, His head covered by a prayer shawl. He took the scroll of Isaiah, opened it, and read to the people: "The Spirit of the Lord is on Me. He has anointed Me to tell the good news to poor people. He has sent Me to announce freedom for prisoners. He has sent Me so that the blind will see again. He wants me to free those who are beaten down. And He has sent Me to announce the year when He will set His people free."

Everyone stared at Jesus. "Today this passage of Scripture is coming true as you listen." By that, Jesus meant that He was the One Isaiah was talking about, the One God had promised to Adam and Eve, Abraham, and David.

Everywhere Jesus went He listened to people others ignored. He saw people others overlooked. He touched people others shunned. And He loved people others hated.

One day, blind Bartimaeus sat alongside the road to Jericho with his stone jar. He was there every day, begging for food and money. Bartimaeus *had* to beg. In those days, there was no other way for the blind to survive.

Suddenly, he heard a crowd coming from the city. Bartimaeus pulled his legs in so no one would step on them and listened carefully. Was the crowd angry, sad, or joyful? That's when he figured it out: Jesus was coming!

Bartimaeus had heard people talk about Jesus. *Maybe today I'll have my chance to meet Jesus*, he thought, *and I won't give up until He stops me*. Bartimaeus listened to the rap of sandals passing until he sensed that Jesus was close. Then he YELLED at the top of his lungs: "Jesus! Son of David! Have mercy on me!"

"Shush," a man nearby said. "Jesus is in a hurry. Besides, He has no money for you."

But Bartimaeus wouldn't. He cried even *louder*, "Son of David! Have mercy on me!"

Jesus stopped. "Call for him," He said.

Now people encouraged Bartimaeus. "Get up on your feet. Jesus is calling for you." Bartimaeus jumped to his feet and felt his way to Jesus.

"What do you want me to do for you?" Jesus asked, touching Bartimaeus' arm to show His nearness. Jesus knew that Bartimaeus didn't want money.

"I want to be able to see," Bartimaeus pleaded.

"Your faith has healed you," Jesus said. Right away, Bartimaeus saw Jesus' face—then the crowd, trees, rocks on the road, dirt, sky. He could *see!* And he began following Jesus. The crowd was amazed.

Another day, a man came and dropped down at Jesus' feet. He threw back his cloak to show the white spots covering his body. Leprosy! Because of this disease, the man had to live outside the city, away from family and friends. No one could touch him. Whenever he saw someone coming, he had to shout, "Unclean!' so they'd go the other way. *Jesus is my last hope*, he thought. *Will He shout and order me away like everyone else?* The man cringed at the thought. "Lord, if You're willing, make me 'clean,'" he begged Jesus.

Jesus reached out His hand and *touched* him. "I am willing," He said. "Be clean!" Right away, the man's skin became soft and the spots left.

You'd think that everyone would be thrilled with Jesus' miracles. But the Pharisees—Jewish religious leaders—were jealous of Jesus. They wanted Him to obey their rules rather than God.

One Sabbath, Jesus noticed a woman leaning wearily on a cane. She was so crippled that she faced the floor when she stood as straight as she could. Jesus called her

gently, "Come here." She hobbled over, twisting her body to look up at Him. "Woman, you will no longer be disabled, Jesus said. "I am about to set you free." Then He put His hands on her. She straightened up, standing tall for the first time in 18 years. Bursting into tears, she praised God.

"There are six days for work," a rough voice growled. It was the synagogue ruler. "Come and be healed on those days. But do not come on the Sabbath."

"You pretenders!" Jesus said. "Doesn't each of you go to the barn and untie his ox or donkey on the Sabbath day? Then don't you lead it out to give it water? This woman is a member of Abraham's family line. But Satan has kept her disabled for 18 long years. Shouldn't she be set free on the Sabbath day from what was keeping her disabled?" The leaders who were against Jesus were embarrassed and angry. But the people knew that God loved them by the wonderful things Jesus did.

Questions:

1. Why do you think Jesus healed people when they asked Him?
2. What do Jesus' healings tell you about how God loves you?

Prayer:

Thank God for caring about your health. Ask God to remind you to pray for yourself and others when they're sick.

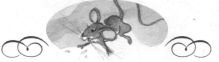

Learning to Walk

(Matthew 5:1–7:28; Luke 6:27–42; John 1:43–50)

Nathanael remembered the day Jesus called him to be His disciple. He'd been standing under a fig tree, looking for ripe figs. *A tree can't have too many figs to suit me*, he'd thought, as he chewed a juicy piece of fruit. *I'll dry some for the winter.* Just then, Philip had run up all excited.

"Nathanael, you've got to come and see!" Philip had said. "We've found the One that Moses wrote about in the Law. The prophets also wrote about Him. He is Jesus of Nazareth, son of Joseph."

"Nazareth?" Nathanael sneered. "Can anything good come from there?" Nathanael thought people from

Nazareth didn't know anything. The Messiah couldn't live *there!* But Philip was a good friend, so Nathanael had gone with him to check it out.

When Jesus saw Nathanael coming, He told Peter, "He is a true Israelite. There is nothing false in him."

"How do you know me?" Nathanael had asked, puzzled. He'd never seen Jesus before this moment. But Jesus knew people's hearts even before He met them.

"I saw you while you were still under the fig tree. I saw you there before Philip called you," Jesus answered.

Nathanael believed in Jesus right away. "You are the Son of God. You are the King of Israel," he said. He decided to follow Jesus and learn how to walk in God's ways.

Nathanael found that Jesus didn't just teach rules like other rabbis. He taught about the way God saw things, and about people's hearts. The Pharisees scolded others to keep the Law, but Jesus knew that the Pharisees didn't see their own sins. "You look at the bit of sawdust in your friend's eye," Jesus said. "But you pay no attention to the piece of wood in your own eye. How can you say to your friend, 'Let me take the bit of sawdust out of your eye' while there's a piece of wood in your own eye?. . .First take the piece of wood out of your own eye. Then you will be able to see clearly to take the bit of sawdust out of your friend's eye."

Nathanael grinned. *I get it*, he thought. *God's way is being the same on the inside as you are on the outside. That's how He wants us all to be.*

Crowds gathered around Jesus to hear Him teach

from early morning to late at night. *Jesus must get tired of people always needing something*, Nathanael thought. But Jesus taught, "Blessed are those who are spiritually needy. The kingdom of heaven belongs to them. Blessed are those who are hungry and thirsty for what is right. They will be filled." People who crowded around Jesus to learn from Him didn't bother Jesus. They pleased Him.

The disciples got angry when they saw the religious leaders try to trick Jesus and get Him in trouble. But Jesus taught, "Love your enemies. Pray for those who hurt you. Then you will be sons of your Father who is in heaven."

Once Jesus heard the disciples discussing what food they could buy with little money. He told them gently: "Don't worry about your life and what you will eat or drink. And don't worry about your body and what you will wear. . .But put God's kingdom first. Do what He wants you to do. Then all of those things will also be given to you."

It's true, Nathanael thought. *Every day God makes sure we have food and a place to sleep.*

One day a Pharisee walked into the temple behind a servant blowing a trumpet. The Pharisee held up a sack of money so all could see, then he dropped it into the box for the poor. *Wow! That's a lot of money*, Nathanael thought.

Jesus saw it too. He warned, "Be careful not to do 'good works' in front of others so that they can see you and give you honor. If you do, your Father in heaven won't reward you. . . . And when you pray, go into your room.

Close the door and pray to your Father who can't be seen. He will reward you. Your Father sees what is done secretly."

The more time Nathanael spent with Jesus, the more he wanted to be just like Him. *If I want to know God, there's one thing I need to learn for sure,* he thought. "Lord, teach us how to pray," Nathanael pleaded.

"This is how you should pray," Jesus said. "'Our Father in heaven, may Your name be honored. May Your kingdom come. May what You want to happen be done on earth as it is done in heaven. Give us today our daily bread. Forgive us our sins, just as we also have forgiven those who sin against us. Keep us from falling into sin when we are tempted. Save us from the evil one.'"

"May the power and glory be Yours forever," Nathanael whispered.

Questions:
1. What's your favorite teaching of Jesus'? Why?
2. Which teaching do you think needs more of your attention?

Prayer:
Ask God for help in following what Jesus taught.

The Farmer's Fields

(Matthew 7:24–29; Matthew 9:9–12; Matthew 13:1–23; Mark 4:1–20; Luke 6:47–49; 8:4–15)

Life sure changed when I met Jesus, Matthew thought. *I used to be a lonely man, even if I was a rich one.* Matthew remembered sitting behind his collection table in the town square of Capernaum. Matthew was a tax collector then, and people hated tax collectors. Tax collectors cheated people out of their money. They also worked for the cruel Romans who ruled Israel.

One day, a crowd had gathered in the square. Matthew became curious when he heard an outburst from the rabbis and an "Ahhh," from the crowd. "What's going on?" Matthew asked a man.

"The teachers of the Law got angry when Jesus said a

lame man's sins were forgiven. They said no one could forgive sins but God. But then Jesus healed the man. He got up and walked! I'm going home to tell my wife."

I'd like to be one of Jesus' disciples, Matthew thought suddenly, a lump in his throat. *But Jesus would never choose me, a tax collector.* Suddenly feeling very ashamed of his life, Matthew looked up to see Jesus walking right up to him.

"Follow me," Jesus said. Jesus had forgiven Matthew's sin too, and gave him a chance for a whole new life.

That was quite a day, Matthew grinned. That night, Jesus and His disciples even came to Matthew's house for dinner with some of Matthew's tax collector friends. The Pharisees clucked their tongues and asked why Jesus ate with sinners. *They'd* never do such a thing! But Jesus had answered, "Those who are healthy don't need a doctor. Sick people do. . .I have not come to get those who think they are right with God to follow me. I have come to get sinners to follow me." Of course, Jesus understood what the Pharisees didn't: everyone was a sinner, except Jesus.

Now that Matthew was Jesus' disciple, he followed Jesus everywhere and took notes when Jesus taught. One day Jesus told a story about a farmer. "A farmer went out to plant his seed," He began. "He scattered the seed on the ground. Some fell on a path. Birds came and ate it up. Some seed fell on rocky places, where there wasn't much soil. The plants came up quickly, because the soil wasn't deep. When the sun came up, it burned the plants. They

dried up because they had no roots. Other seed fell among thorns. The thorns grew up and crowded out the plants."

Jesus slowed a little so His words could sink in. "Still other seed fell on good soil. It produced a crop 100, 60, or 30 times more than what was planted. Those who have ears should listen."

Matthew scratched his head. He heard the story, but what did it mean? He asked Jesus, "Why do You use stories when You speak to the people?"

Jesus explained that when He spoke about the kingdom of heaven, most people looked but didn't see. They heard but didn't understand. They would easily remember His stories later—when they were able to understand.

"The seed is God's message," Jesus explained. "People on the path are those who hear. But then the devil comes. He takes away the message from their hearts. He does it so they won't believe. Then they can't be saved.

"Those on the rock are the ones who hear the message and receive it with joy. But they have no roots. They believe for a while. But when they are put to the test, they fall away from the faith.

"The seed that fell among thorns stands for those who hear the message. But as they go on their way, they are choked by life's worries, riches and pleasures. So they do not reach full growth.

"But the seed on good soil stands for those with an honest and good heart. They hear the message. They

keep it in their hearts. They remain faithful and produce a good crop."

Matthew nodded, his eyes teary. *God changed my heart and made it good ground*, he thought.

"So then, everyone who hears my words and puts them into practice is like a wise man," Jesus said. "He builds his house on the rock. The rain comes down. The water rises. The winds blow and beat against that house. But it does not fall. It is built on the rock.

"But everyone who hears My words and does not put them into practice is like a foolish man. He builds his house on sand. The rain comes down. The water rises. The winds blow and beat against that house. And it falls with a loud crash."

Matthew took Jesus' words into his heart and they changed the way he lived—forever.

Questions:

1. Some stories are easy to remember. What are your favorites?
2. What things could you do to "build your house on rock?"

Prayer:

Ask for God's help to understand Jesus' teaching and to make your heart like good soil.

The Samaritan's Story

(Luke 10:25–37)

The teacher rolled up his scroll and got up from his chair to stretch. He was an expert in the Law. He'd been studying all week. Now he was ready. People used to crowd around him in the temple and ask him for answers. Now they crowded around Jesus. *It's the same way all over Galilee*, he thought, *and it has to stop!*

It wasn't hard to find Jesus. You only had to look for the crowd; Jesus would be in the middle. The expert in the Law stood with his arms crossed, waiting for his opportunity. He had the perfect question to trap Jesus. He cleared his throat, then asked loudly, "Teacher, what must I do to receive eternal life?" The crowd turned toward him. It was the most important question on all their hearts.

Jesus looked at the man carefully, then asked him, "What is written in the Law? How do you understand it?"

The teacher was delighted. This gave him a chance to answer his own question for the crowd. He answered, "'Love the LORD your God with all your heart and with all your soul. Love Him with all your strength and with all your mind.' And, 'Love your neighbor as you love yourself.'" His answer came straight from the scriptures.

"You have answered correctly," Jesus said. "Do that, and you will live."

The expert of the Law decided to take it one step further to show off his own knowledge. "And who is my neighbor?" he asked in liquid tones. Surely, Jesus would stumble on this one. The teacher had studied all night to come up with the correct answer.

Jesus knew the teacher's heart. He knew the man wanted to make Him look bad. This time, He did not turn the question back to him, but told a story instead.

"A man was going down from Jerusalem to Jericho," Jesus began. "Robbers attacked him. They stripped off his clothes and beat him. Then they went away, leaving him almost dead. A priest happened to be going down that same road. When he saw the man, he passed by on the other side."

Of course, the expert on the Law thought, planning his next step in the discussion. *The priest didn't want to make himself unclean by touching a dead body. That's the Law.* He was just ready to tell the crowd that, but Jesus continued with His story.

"A Levite also came by," Jesus said. "When he saw the man, he passed by on the other side too."

Hmm, a Levite? The expert thought. *How can I explain that one? It's not as clear. . .*

Jesus looked the teacher in the eyes. Although he wanted to trick Jesus, Jesus loved the man and wanted to touch his heart with God's message. So He finished the story.

"But a Samaritan came to the place where the man was. When he saw the man, he felt sorry for him. He went to him, poured olive oil and wine on his wounds and bandaged them. Then he put the man on his own donkey. He took him to an inn and took care of him.

"The next day he took out two silver coins. He gave them to the owner of the inn. 'Take care of him,' he said. 'When I return, I will pay you back for any extra expense you may have."

"Which of the three do you think was a neighbor to the man who was attacked by robbers?" Jesus asked the expert on the Law.

The teacher stiffened. He was cornered. Jesus' story suggested that a *Samaritan*—a hated enemy of the Jews—was better than a priest and a Levite. But he couldn't

answer any other way. "The one who felt sorry for him,' he muttered, his eyes flashing in anger.

Jesus told him, "Go and do as he did."

The expert on the Law walked away, silent. Jesus had hoped to soften the man's hard heart. Perhaps one day he'd really understand the truth of God's love for everyone.

Questions:

1. Why do you think the Samaritan stopped to help a man he didn't even know?
2. What are some ways you can be a neighbor to your family and friends?

Prayer:

Ask God for help to be a good neighbor by being kind and helpful to everyone, especially those in need.

Born Twice?

(John 3:1–20)

Nicodemus gathered his cloak around his roundish figure and glanced nervously down the dark street. Then he stood tall (which wasn't very tall at all). *Pharisees don't skulk around,* he told himself. *We're well respected. We can go anywhere.* But he was going to see Someone other Pharisees wouldn't be caught dead visiting: Jesus. Nicodemus had to admit he was a little nervous.

Who is He? Nicodemus wondered. *No ordinary man, from all I hear. Certainly, He's a great teacher. But is that all? I need to find out. . . . no matter what the other Pharisees think. But I hope they don't learn about this secret visit.*

He paused at the edge of a garden. The moon threw

silver light over the trees, bushes, and grass. A light breeze stirred leaves and ruffled his robe. Suddenly a huge shadow rose up. Nicodemus jumped.

"What do you want?" It was Andrew, one of Jesus' disciples.

Nicodemus drew himself up proudly to show his high position. "Take me to Jesus," he said firmly.

The man turned without a word and led him to where Jesus sat beneath an olive tree.

"Rabbi," Nicodemus began politely, seating himself. "We know you are a teacher who has come from God. We know that God is with You. If He weren't, you couldn't do the miraculous signs you are doing." Nicodemus furrowed his brow as he leaned forward on the edge of his chair. Jesus knew he wasn't asking the question on behalf of all the Pharisees. Nicodemus really wanted to understand for himself.

"The truth is," Jesus replied, "no one can see God's kingdom without being born again."

Nicodemus was confused—and a little scared. He didn't know what Jesus was talking about. He wasn't used to being the one who didn't understand! The safest thing was to ask another question.

"How can I be born when I am old?" he asked Jesus. It seemed like nonsense to him. "I can't go back inside my mother! I can't be born a second time!" He straightened up on his chair and leaned back a bit. *Maybe we can start over on a safer subject*, he thought.

But Jesus knew that Nicodemus, unlike most other

Pharisees, was ready to learn the truth about Him. "I tell you the truth," Jesus replied. "No one can enter God's kingdom without being born through water and the Holy Spirit. People give birth to people. But the Spirit gives birth to spirit."

Nicodemus sat silent for a long time. *This is a deep thing*, he thought.

"The wind blows where it wants to," Jesus continued, waving at the dancing branches above them. "You hear its sound but you can't tell where it comes from or where it's going. It's the same with everyone born through the Spirit." Jesus was telling Nicodemus God's Spirit was something Nicodemus couldn't control, any more than he could control the wind.

"How can this be?" Nicodemus asked softly.

"You are Israel's teacher. Don't you understand these things?" Jesus gently scolded. The Pharisees tried to teach others about things they didn't understand themselves. "I have spoken to you about earthly things, and you do not believe," Jesus pointed out. "So how will you believe if I speak about heavenly things?"

Jesus looked at Nicodemus with great love. "God loved the world so much that He gave His one and only Son. Anyone who believes in Him will not die, but will have eternal life."

God's Son? Nicodemus thought, alarmed. *Is Jesus saying He's God's Son?* Nicodemus' thoughts were spinning.

Jesus was almost finished. "God did not send His

Son into the world to judge the world." He explained. "He sent His Son to save the world through Him. Anyone who believes in Him is not judged. But anyone who does not believe is judged already. He has not believed in the name of God's one and only Son."

So there it was: the complete story. Jesus claimed to be God's Only Son. Nicodemus wasn't sure whether to run, rage, or fall at Jesus' feet in worship. One thing was certain. Now that he knew, Nicodemus had to make a choice.

Nicodemus got up without a word and slowly headed home. He had much to think and pray about. He mustn't make a mistake! Jesus' words echoed through his heart. "Anyone who *believes in Him. . .*"

Questions:

1. Why do you think Nicodemus came to see Jesus at night rather than during the daytime?
2. John 3:16 says, "God loved the world so much that He gave His one and only Son. Anyone who believes in Him won't die, but will have eternal life." What does this verse mean to you?

Prayer:

Thank God for sending Jesus so that you can be His child.

Children's Huddle

(Matthew 18:1–6; 19:13–15; Mark 9:33–37; 10:13–16; Luke 9:46–48; 18:15–17)

Jesus stopped to wipe His forehead and sip some water. He was walking ahead of the group today to think and pray. Soon the Pharisees would stop Him from teaching, and His disciples still had much to learn.

Jesus looked back down the road. The disciples waved their arms in the air and shook their fingers to make their point as they talked. Jesus sighed. He knew what they were discussing. All the crowd's talk of making Him king had gotten them off track. When they got to Capernaum, He'd have to correct them. *How can I help them understand, Father?* He prayed.

Later, as they rested in Capernaum, Jesus asked

them, "What were you arguing about on the road?"

No one answered. They just shuffled their feet. They knew that Jesus wouldn't be happy to hear they'd been arguing about who was most important. But Jesus didn't need to be told. He already knew.

"If you want to be first, you must be the very last," Jesus said. "You must be the servant of everyone." The disciples looked at one another. That didn't make sense to them. Weren't important people the ones that everyone else served?

Jesus looked around. A small boy had crawled under benches and around the disciples' legs to sit on a nearby rock where he could watch Jesus' face. Jesus winked and crooked a finger at him. The boy ran to Jesus, grinning as if he'd won a huge prize. Then Jesus lifted him onto His lap, ruffled his hair and tickled him. Both of them laughed. It was wonderful to be in Jesus' arms and snuggle close to Him!

"The truth is," Jesus said to His disciples, "you need to change and become like little children." The boy looked into Jesus' face, and reached up to pat His beard. He trusted Jesus completely. "If you don't," Jesus continued, "you will never enter the kingdom of heaven. Anyone who becomes as free of pride as this child is the most important in the kingdom of heaven."

Jesus saw the disciples' puzzled looks. They all loved children. But in those days, it was men first, women second, and children last. Jesus wanted them to be like

children? How could they do that?

"Anyone who welcomes one of these little children in My name welcomes Me," Jesus continued, kissing the boy's hair. "And anyone who welcomes Me doesn't welcome only Me but also the One who sent Me."

The disciples looked lost. Jesus needed to teach them again, another way. He put the child back on his feet and sent him to his mother who'd just come to see what was going on. She beamed when she saw her son with Jesus.

The next day Jesus taught from a hill outside town. As always, people surrounded Him. Mothers with young children pushed their way through the crowds to get close. Maybe they'd heard how Jesus had taken a child in His lap the day before. All the children begged to touch Jesus and hug Him.

Jesus looked tired and hot. The disciples seemed worried and were shooing people away. "Stop!" James frowned, barring the way of one woman and her son with his arm. "Go back."

The boy's face crumpled and tears rolled down his cheeks as he clung tightly to his mom. She started to speak then looked down, near tears herself. She patted her son's head and shifted the baby in her arms. "Not today," she told them, turning sadly away.

"Wait!" a voice called. Jesus walked toward them. The boy grinned and ran to Him, taking His hand. Jesus squeezed it, then turned to the disciples. "Let the little

children come to Me," He said. "Don't keep them away." He knelt down and held out His arms with a big smile. All through the crowd, children broke loose from their parents and ran to Jesus. Soon they were one big huddle around Him, almost knocking Him off His feet in excitement. Jesus laughed, His eyes no longer tired. He hugged each one in turn and blessed them.

The disciples watched silently. Children were important to Jesus. He wanted to be with them as much as they did. And Jesus didn't want anyone to get in the way of that. *He stopped teaching to serve the smallest and least important in the crowd*, James realized, *just as He taught us to do.*

Questions:

1. Have you ever tried to get through a crowd to see someone famous? What do you think it was like for those kids and parents trying to see Jesus?
2. Jesus showed everyone that He loves children. How do you know He loves you?

Prayer:

Thank God for loving you. Ask for help to let other children know how much He loves them.

Plans and Traps

(Matthew 22:15–22; Mark 12:13–17; Luke 20:20–26; John 7:45–52; 8:1–11; 10:22–42; 11:49–52)

L ook at that!" a tall Pharisee growled, standing at the edge of the crowd. "The people hang on every word He says. It's disgusting! They never listen to us that way."

His companion nodded grimly, stroking his beard, "If the crowds get too excited, the Romans might think we're rebelling against them. They'll clamp down on us and take away the power we've worked so hard to get. This man has to be stopped." The others in the group muttered agreement as they glowered at Jesus. "I have a plan," one said, leading them to a quiet corner of the temple. As he laid it out, frowns turned to sly smiles.

"Excellent!" the tall Pharisee smirked. "We'll trap Him with His own words! I know just the men who could do it."

The next day, several young men approached Jesus. "Teacher," one said respectfully, "we know You are a man of honor. You don't let others tell You what to do or say. You don't care how important they are. But You teach the way of God truthfully. Is it right to pay taxes to Caesar or not?"

Jesus knew what they were trying to do. If He said yes, the people might turn on Him. They hated the Roman tax, and argued that Rome had no right to tax them. But if Jesus said no, the Romans could accuse Him of speaking against their government. "Why are you trying to trap Me?" He asked, looking from one to the other until they blushed. "Bring Me a silver coin. Let Me look at it."

One of them handed Jesus a Roman coin, so different from their simple Jewish coins. "Whose picture is this?" Jesus asked, holding up the engraved piece of silver.

"Caesar's," they answered.

"Give to Caesar what belongs to Caesar," Jesus said. He pinned each man with His eyes, "And give to God what belongs to God." They'd have to decide themselves what belonged to whom. Amazed with Jesus' answer, they walked away.

A few days later, as Jesus taught in the temple, some

Pharisees and teachers of the Law dragged in a woman they had caught in sin. One of the men flung her roughly toward Jesus, saying, "Teacher, we caught her in sin. The Law of Moses says she should be stoned for that sin. What do You say?"

Jesus bent down and wrote on the ground with His finger. He knew this was another trap.

Confused, the man kept repeating his question.

Jesus loved these people, even His enemies. He'd try again to get through to them. Straightening, He looked from one to another. "Has any one of you not sinned? Then you be the first to throw a stone at her." Then He stooped down and wrote on the ground again.

The people shifted uncomfortably, remembering sins they'd committed. The oldest dropped his stone first and walked away. Others followed. Soon, the woman stood alone, weeping. Jesus stood up and asked her gently, "Where are they? Is there anyone left to punish you?"

"No one, sir," she answered.

"Then neither will I," Jesus said. "Go now, and leave your life of sin."

Another trap foiled! But the Pharisees weren't done. One day when Jesus arrived at the temple, a crowd, stirred up by the Pharisees, surrounded Him.

"How long will you keep us waiting?" they asked. "If You are the Christ, tell us plainly."

Jesus answered them, with love. "I did tell you. . .The kinds of things I do in My Father's name speak for Me.

But you do not believe," He explained sadly, "because you are not My sheep. My sheep listen to My voice. . .and they follow Me. No one can steal them out of My hand. . .My Father, who has given them to Me, is greater than anyone. . .I and the Father are one."

By now, the Pharisees were beside themselves with fear and rage. "You're making yourself out to be God!" they shouted. And they picked up stones to kill Him. But Jesus slipped away.

From that day on, the Pharisees planned to kill Jesus and looked for ways to get Him away from the crowds.

Questions:

1. Why do you think none of these traps worked?
2. How should we act toward people who don't believe in Jesus?

Prayer:

Ask God for wisdom to be gentle and nice to people who don't believe in Jesus.

Jesus' Last Meal

(Matthew 26:2–5, 14–35;
Mark 14:1–2, 10–11,12–31;
Luke 22:1–23, 31–34;
John 11:50, 12:6, 13:1–30)

Soon many thousands of people would flood the already bustling city of Jerusalem for the feast of the Passover. "If we arrest Jesus with the Passover crowds around, they'll riot." High Priest Caiaphas warned. The chief priests and elders nodded. They plotted the best way to get rid of Jesus once and for all. But some weren't so sure, thinking of Jesus' miracles.

"You don't realize what's good for you," Caiaphas cried. "It's better if one man dies for the people than if the whole nation's destroyed!" And with that, It was settled.

Not long after, while Jesus and His disciples ate dinner, a woman came and poured expensive perfume over Him. "Why wasn't this perfume sold?" Judas Iscariot complained. "Why wasn't the money given to poor people? It was worth a year's pay." Judas didn't really care about the poor. He was the disciple in charge of the group's money, and often stole from it.

But Jesus defended the woman, saying she had done a good thing. *That's the last straw! Judas thought, disgusted. I expected to rule with Jesus, but He talks about dying instead of becoming king. And now this!*

Evil had crept into Judas' heart. He snuck away to meet with the religious leaders, knowing they were Jesus' enemies. The guards showed Judas into a beautiful meeting room with marble floors, plush chairs, and gorgeous tapestries. *If things go my way*, he thought, *I'll soon have such things, too.* He turned to the leaders. "What will you give me if I hand Jesus over to you?"

The Pharisees were all smiles. This was just what they'd been waiting for. They haggled briefly, then settled on thirty pieces of silver. Judas dropped the money into his pocket and promised to watch for the right time to hand Jesus over to them.

The evening of Passover, Judas took his place with the rest of the disciples reclining on couches around a low table. "I have really looked forward to eating this Passover meal with you. I wanted to do this before I suffer," Jesus told them. Then He took some bread, thanked God and broke it. Handing pieces to the disciples, He said, "This is My body. It is given for you.

Every time you eat it, do it in memory of Me."

Then He took a cup of wine, saying, "This cup is the new covenant in my blood. It is poured out for you."

After the meal, Jesus got up from the table and took off His robe. Then He wrapped a towel around His waist, and washed each disciple's feet. *Now Jesus is doing the work of a lowly servant!* Judas thought.

"Do you understand what I have done for you?" Jesus asked when He'd finished. "You call me 'Teacher' and 'Lord.' You are right. That is what I am. I, your Lord and Teacher, have washed your feet. So you also should wash one another's feet." Jesus wasn't talking just about washing feet. He meant they should care for one another in all kinds of ways, just as He had cared for them.

Then Jesus looked at His friends around the table and became troubled. Judas held his breath. *Does Jesus know?*

"One of you is going to hand me over to My enemies," Jesus said, His voice filled with pain.

Judas let his breath out slowly. *It's as good as done now*, he thought.

The other disciples shouted. "No! Who? It can't be me, can it, Lord?"

John, sitting next to Jesus, leaned back on Jesus' chest and asked quietly, "Lord, who is it?"

"It is the one I will give this piece of bread to," Jesus whispered in John's ear. Then He gave the bread to Judas.

"Do quickly what you are going to do." Jesus said.

Judas hurried out into the night.

"You will all turn away," Jesus told the others sadly.

Peter disagreed. "All the others may turn away. But I will not."

"It will happen today, this very night." Jesus answered. "Before the rooster crows twice, you yourself will say three times that you don't know Me." Peter was speechless.

Knowing this was His last chance to teach His disciples before He died, Jesus told them about His Father and how much He wanted them to love one other. "You must love one another, just as I have loved you," Jesus said. "If you love one another, everyone will know you are My disciples."

Questions:

1. How do you think the disciples felt when Jesus was washing their feet? Why?
2. Have you ever been in a church meeting that used the symbols of bread and wine that Jesus used? Talk about how they can help you remember what Jesus did.

Prayer:

Ask God to help you follow His example in helping and giving to others every day.

Betrayed!

(Matthew 26:36–55; Mark 14:32–52; Luke 22:39–53; John 18:1–11)

"Come with Me," Jesus said to Peter, James, and John. They left the other disciples under the olive trees in the garden called Gethsemane on the Mount of Olives. They disappeared in the shadows beneath the trees.

"My soul is very sad," Jesus told His friends, His voice choked. "Stay here. Keep watch with Me."

Jesus walked a little further then fell with His face to the ground in prayer. He knew what was coming. "My Father," He prayed, "if it is possible, take this cup of suffering away from Me." He groaned as He added, "But let what You want be done, not what I want."

The three watched Jesus, unsure what to do. They'd never seen Him like this. Finally, they sat, leaning against rocks or tree trunks. They prayed for a while but it was getting late. Soon they gave in to the quiet of the garden.

Later Jesus came back to Peter, James, and John. They were asleep! Peter startled awake. "Couldn't you men keep watch with Me for one hour?" Jesus asked him. "Watch and pray. . . .The spirit is willing, but the body is weak."

Peter remembered Jesus had said he would deny Him. He was determined not to let Jesus down, but he still dozed off.

Jesus went back to pray the same thing. Again, He agreed to do whatever God wanted. But it was very hard. When Jesus returned, the three friends were still sleeping. They couldn't keep their eyes open. He let them sleep this time and He went back to pray even harder.

Jesus knew that taking everyone's sins on Himself would be horrible! But He also knew God's way was best. He prayed so hard that His sweat was like drops of blood. Finally, Jesus prayed for strength and an angel from heaven appeared to strengthen Him. Then peace came. He was ready.

"Are you still sleeping?" Jesus asked when He returned to His friends. "Get Up! . . .Here comes the one who is handing me over to them!"

Judas walked into the garden followed by a squad of Roman soldiers, some temple guards, and a few leaders. Armed with swords and clubs, the men carried lanterns and torches so they could find Jesus if He tried to hide among the trees. Judas smiled. The flickering torchlight made him look evil.

"Greetings, Rabbi," he said, stepping forward to kiss Jesus. That was Judas' sign that He was the Man to arrest.

"Judas, "Jesus said, "are you handing over the Son of Man with a kiss?" Then He turned to the crowd. "Who is it that you want?"

"Jesus of Nazareth."

"I am He." When they heard this, the soldiers and guards fell back. "If you are looking for Me, then let these men go." Jesus said.

Men stepped forward. Suddenly Peter jumped in front of Jesus. "NO!" he yelled, and he cut off the ear of the high priest's servant, Malchus. Malchus screamed, clutching the side of his head.

"Put your sword back in its place," Jesus commanded. He gently touched Malchus' head. When He stepped back, the ear was healed!

"Do you think that I can't ask my Father for help?" Jesus asked Peter, "He would send an army of more than 70,000 angels right away. But then how would the Scriptures come true?" His gaze caught and held the religious leaders. "They say it must happen in this way."

Jesus laughed sadly. "Am I leading a band of armed men against you? Do you have to come with swords and clubs?" He held out His hands for the soldiers to tie and He followed them out of the garden.

Questions:

1. The religious leaders' other traps didn't work. Why do you think this one did?
2. Jesus told God what He wanted, but He trusted God enough to know that His will was best. How can you show God this same trust when you pray?

Prayer:

Thank God that His way is best. Ask for His help to talk to Him about everything, tell Him what you want, but still trust Him that His way is the best way.

Phony Trial, Real Crucifixion

(Matthew 26:57–27:56; Mark 14:53–15:41; Luke 22:54–23:49; John 18:12–19:37)

Pilate heard feet clomping through the empty streets even before the pounding on his door. His worst fears were coming true. Jerusalem was jammed with strangers for something called "Passover," and now there was trouble. If the crowd got out of hand, he could lose his job as Roman governor—or worse. He was relieved to see only the Jewish leaders with a Man tied up in ropes. *One of their silly religious arguments again*, he thought. *Might as well take care of it right away and go back to bed.*

The leaders of the Jews had brought Jesus before their own court after they'd dragged Him from the Garden of Gethsemane. "He deserves to die!" they'd shouted, hitting

Jesus and spitting on Him. (Of course, they'd planned to kill Him from the beginning.) The temple guards had insulted Jesus, punched Him, and laughed at Him. Now at dawn, they brought Him to Pilate.

"This Jesus says He's a king," they said, hoping to convince Pilate that Jesus was a traitor to Rome.

If that were true, I'd be in trouble, Pilate thought. *But I think they're just jealous of Jesus.* "I find no basis for a charge against this man," Pilate said after listening to their claims. "Take Him to Herod. He's in charge of Galilee. Let him decide."

That was clever of me, Pilate congratulated himself, shuffling back to his bedroom. But soon, the Jews returned. By now, they'd gathered a large crowd to help them. "Crucify Him! Crucify Him!" the crowd shouted.

Pilate frowned. *I can't sleep with all this*, he thought. "Let me talk to Jesus myself," he said, signaling the guards to bring Jesus into his palace.

"Why have your own people brought you to me? What have you done?" Pilate asked when they were alone. "Are you the king of the Jews?"

"My kingdom is not part of this world," Jesus said. "But you are right today I am a king. In fact, that's the reason I was born. I came into the world to give witness to the truth. Everyone who is on the side of truth listens to Me."

Pilate looked at Jesus' battered face. *I don't understand this Man*, he thought, *but He's no criminal deserving death. Maybe there's another way to save Him.* Pilate went back to

the crowd outside.

"I can release one prisoner at Passover time," he said. Do you want me to set 'the king of the Jews' free?"

"No!" the crowd roared. "Barabbas! Give us Barabbas!" (Barabbas was in prison for starting a rebellion.)

What's wrong with them? Pilate fumed, heading back inside. He had Jesus whipped. The soldiers shoved a crown made of thorns on Jesus' head and dressed Him in purple robes. "Hail, king," they laughed, bowing before Him, then punching His face time after time. When they'd finished, Pilate took Jesus outside to the crowd. Maybe they'd have pity when they saw Him now.

But the crowd only shouted louder, "Kill Him! Crucify Him!"

Finally, Pilate gave in and handed Jesus over to be crucified. He had the soldiers make a sign to put on the cross above Jesus' head. It read, JESUS OF NAZARETH, THE KING OF THE JEWS. When the chief priests saw it they argued, "It should say this man *claimed* to be king of the Jews."

"I have written what I have written," Pilate answered.

Soldiers forced Jesus to carry a heavy wooden cross to a hill just outside the city called Golgotha, the "Place of the Skull." Then they pounded huge nails through Jesus' hands and ankles, pinning Him to the wood. He was in horrible pain. Yet even now, people tormented Him. "If you're the Son of God, come down off that cross and save yourself."

But Jesus stayed there because He loved us so much that He wanted to make things right with God for *us*. He wanted to end our separation from God caused by sin. He stayed there to "crush the serpent's head," just as God had promised Adam and Eve.

Darkness covered the whole land from noon to three o'clock as Jesus suffered. Finally He said, "Father, into Your hands I commit My very life." He took a deep breath, cried, "It is finished!" then bowed His head and died.

One of the soldiers, seeing how Jesus died, said, "Surely, this was the Son of God!"

Questions:

1. Why do you think Pilate allowed the crowd to have its way?
2. How do you feel when God forgives you for your sins and mistakes?

Prayer:

If you believe this story, tell God. Ask for forgiveness and ask Jesus to come live in your heart.

The Empty Tomb

(Matthew 27:57–28:20; Mark 15:42–16:20; Luke 23:50–24:53; John 19:38–21:25)

Joseph of Arimathea left Pilate's palace to find Nicodemus. (This was the same Nicodemus who'd come to Jesus one night.) "Pilate has agreed," Joseph said. "Romans usually don't let people bury someone who's been crucified. God's with us." They hurried toward Golgotha, where Jesus still hung on the cross. They'd been afraid to admit they believed in Jesus when He was alive. At least they'd show more courage now.

Carefully, the men took Jesus' body down and carried it to a new tomb in a nearby garden. Then they wrapped the body in linen cloths layered with spices and tied a head cloth around His jaw. They had to hurry.

Soon Sabbath would begin. They helped the servants roll a huge stone in front of the tomb's entrance and returned to the city. Mary Magdalene and Mary the mother of Jeses had watched them from a distance, crying. Then they too went home to rest on the Sabbath day in order to obey the Law.

The next morning the chief priests and Pharisees went to Pilate. "Jesus claimed He would rise after three days," they said sneering. "Of course that's a lie. Give the order to guard the tomb until the third day. Otherwise His disciples may steal His body and tell people He's risen from the dead."

Pilate rolled his eyes. He was tired of the whole thing. "Fine," he said. "Take some guards with you. Go. Make the tomb as secure as you can."

So they sealed the stone with wax and left Roman soldiers to guard it. *Now* if anyone came to cause mischief, they'd never get away with it! But the leaders needn't have worried. Jesus' disciples were shaken to the core by Jesus' death, and feared they might be next. They were all in hiding.

Early on the third day, Mary Magdalene and some other women went to the tomb. In their grief, they didn't notice the dawn sky painted pink, the birds singing, or the light breeze dancing with the tree leaves.

Suddenly the ground shook. Birds took off screeching as the women stumbled. In the garden, an angel that shone like lightning came down from heaven and rolled

away the stone. Terrified, the Roman guards shook and became like dead men.

As soon as they regained their footing, the women rushed toward the garden. Seeing the angel, they were frightened and bowed their faces to the ground. The angel said to them, "I know you're looking for Jesus who was crucified. He's not here! He's risen just as He said He would. Come." He waved toward the tomb. "Come and see where He was lying."

It was true! The tomb was empty! The linen strips that Joseph and Nicodemus used to wrap His body were lying by themselves. Then the women remembered what Jesus had told them.

Still shaking but full of joy, they hurried back to tell the disciples the glorious news. But the disciples didn't believe them.

Meanwhile, the Roman guards ran to tell the chief priests what they'd seen. The chief priests slumped in their chairs. *How could this happen after they'd been so careful?* They didn't really listen to what the guards described or even see the wonder on their faces. Offering the Romans a large sum of money, they instructed them, "Say that Jesus' disciples came during the night and stole His body while you were sleeping. If Pilate hears, we'll make sure you don't get in trouble."

The soldiers knew their officers wouldn't believe the truth. They weren't sure they did! So they kept the money.

That evening, the disciples gathered in a small room

in Jerusalem. They'd locked the doors because they were afraid of the Jews. Suddenly Jesus came in and stood among them! He showed them His hands and His side. Their mouths dropped open and their eyes grew large in amazement. Then they grinned and cheered and praised God! Everything Jesus had said was true!

Jesus was *alive!* He appeared several more times around Galilee, proving beyond any doubt that He was risen from the dead.

Questions:

1. Imagine being one of the first to see Jesus alive after you knew He was dead. What would you see? What would you feel?

2. Death couldn't keep Jesus because He had no sin. He paid for *our* sins. Talk about how, once your sins are forgiven, death can't keep you either.

Prayer:

Thank Jesus for rising from the dead and giving you eternal life.

Jesus Returns to Heaven

(Matthew 28:16–20; Mark 16:14–20; Luke 24:36–52; John 19–21:25; Acts 1:1–11)

L ast week Jesus appeared right here," Thaddaeus told Thomas, his eyes shining. "He said He's sending us just as the Father sent Him."

Thomas Didymus was one of Jesus' disciples, but he hadn't been in this room with the others the week before. "I'd like to believe you, Thaddaeus," he said, "but it's so, so...well, it's just impossible. First I must see the nail marks in His hands. I must put my finger where the nails were. I must put my hand into His side. Only then will I believe what you say."

Suddenly a familiar voice said, "May peace be with you." A sweet calm flooded the now silent room. It was Jesus! He smiled and then turned toward Thomas,

387

"Thomas, come," Jesus said. "Put your finger here. See My hands. Reach out your hand and put it into My side. Stop doubting and believe."

Thomas felt a tumble of emotions—embarrassment, fear, joy. Then his doubts vanished as his heart flooded with faith. He cried, "My Lord and my God!" and he dropped to his knees before Jesus.

Jesus put His hand on Thomas' shoulder. "Because you have seen Me, you believe. Blessed are those who have not seen Me yet still have believed."

Later one evening in Galilee, Peter said, "I'm going fishing!" Thomas, Nathanael, James, and John joined him as he got the boat ready. All night the friends talked about Jesus as they fished.

Toward morning, Peter grew very quiet. "Anything wrong?" James asked him.

"There's something I've never told anyone," Peter said, swallowing hard. "But I just can't get it out of my mind. Remember when Jesus said that I'd deny Him—the night He got arrested?"

The others nodded. Who could forget that night? Jesus had told Peter, "Before the rooster crows you'll deny me three times."

Peter began to unfold the whole story. "Well, when the mob took Jesus from the garden to the High Priest's house, I followed them from a distance into Caiaphas' courtyard." Peter closed his eyes a moment. In his mind, he still heard people laughing and shouting at Jesus, then punching Him. Peter shivered at the memory.

"One servant girl had noticed me and said, 'You were

with this Jesus. "But I told her I didn't know what she was talking about. Later, two others thought they recognized me as Jesus' disciple. I told them I didn't even know the Man!" Peter stopped again, tears streaming. "When a rooster crowed, I realized what I'd done."

No one knew what to say. None of them was proud of their behavior that night.

Soon the sky turned pink. Time to head back. Though they'd fished the whole night, their nets were empty. As they neared the shore, someone appeared out of the morning mist.

"Friends, don't you have any fish?" He called.

"No," they answered.

"Throw your net on the right side of the boat. There you will find some fish."

Shrugging, they did as He said. The net was so full they couldn't drag it back aboard. John peered toward the shore. "It's the Lord!" he grinned. Peter grabbed his coat and jumped into the water, swimming to Jesus.

The smell of cooking fish greeted the others when they reached shore. Jesus was cooking. After they'd eaten, Jesus turned to Peter. "Simon, son of John, do you really love Me?" Three times, He asked the same question—the same number of times Peter had denied Him.

Three times Peter answered, "Yes, Lord. You know I love You."

"Feed My sheep," Jesus said. Then with a soft smile He added, "Follow Me." Those were the same words He'd used to call Peter as His disciple so long ago. Peter grinned in joy: Now he knew Jesus had forgiven him.

Not long after, Jesus led His disciples to the Mount of Olives. Climbing the wooded hill, they asked Jesus, "Are You going to give the kingdom back to Israel now?"

Jesus shook His head. "You should not be concerned about times or dates. . . .But you will receive power when the Holy Spirit comes on you. Then you will be my witnesses in Jerusalem. You will be my witnesses in all Judea and Samaria. And you will be my witnesses from one end of the earth to the other." Jesus was giving them a new job to tell others about Him—and not just Israel, but the whole world.

Then Jesus rose slowly into the air. The disciples watched until a cloud hid Him. Suddenly two men in white stood beside them. "Why do you stand here looking at the sky?" they asked. "Jesus has been taken away from you into heaven. But He will come back in the same way you saw Him go." Full of joy, the disciples returned to Jerusalem to wait for God's promised gift of the Spirit.

Questions:

1. What did Jesus say He wanted the disciples to do after He left?

2. What can you do to be ready to tell others about Jesus?

Prayer:

Ask God to help Christians around the world to tell others about Him.

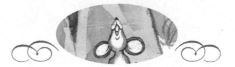

Tongues of Fire!

(Acts 2:1–42; 4:23–37)

Peter and John pushed through the crowds in Jerusalem. It had been almost 50 days since Jesus' crucifixion. Here and there, the two disciples overheard people talk about rumors that Jesus, miracle worker and prophet, had risen from the dead.

"One of the guards said Jesus' disciples stole His body while they were sleeping," a man said.

His friend snorted. "The Romans kill any guards who sleep on duty. If their story's true, why are they still alive?"

"Yeah," added another. "And you can't tell me a bunch of fishermen won a fight with tough soldiers!" They all laughed at the idea.

As Peter and John wove through groups of foreigners in Jerusalem to celebrate the Feast of Pentecost, the unfamiliar languages made them jumpy. What if someone were talking about them? Then a sudden shout made the two whirl toward the noise. They were still afraid the religious leaders might be looking for them. Who knows? There might even be a reward for anyone finding them. Shrinking into the shadows, they forced themselves to walk at a normal pace so they wouldn't draw attention. Finally, breathing sighs of relief, they reached the upper room, the disciples' base of operations as they waited for God's promise.

"Not everyone believes the lies," Peter reported to the others. "After all, over 500 people saw Jesus after He had risen. But it's still not safe. We need to pray more than ever." So the tiny gathering of 120 believers prayed all night for God's Holy Spirit to bring the courage they needed.

The next morning James, John's brother, opened the shutters a crack to let in the cool morning air, then rejoined the group. Suddenly, at 9:00 o'clock, a sound from heaven like a strong wind filled the whole house. The believers fell to their knees as they took in the sound. *He* was there! Then they saw something like tongues of fire settling on each of them. All of them— every single one—were filled with the Holy Spirit and began speaking in languages they hadn't known before. Suddenly, they wanted to share the good news of Jesus

with *everyone!* No more hiding fearfully behind locked doors.

The believers went outside. A crowd had gathered at their door to see what had caused the strange sound of wind. There were people from many different lands. When the believers spoke, the people were amazed. Each of them heard the disciples speaking of God's wonders in their own native language. How could uneducated Galileans do this? It was a miracle.

But others dismissed the marvel saying, "Bah! They've had too much wine!"

Calling for quiet, Peter spoke to the crowd and explained what the prophet Joel had written long ago: "'In the last days,' God says, 'I will pour out My Holy Spirit on all people. Your sons and daughters will prophesy. Your young men will see visions. Your old men will have dreams.'"

Peter boldly told how Jesus fulfilled God's prophecies of the Messiah. "With the help of evil people, you put Jesus to death. You nailed Him to the cross. But God raised Him from the dead." Peter didn't have to prove Jesus' tomb was empty—the crowd already knew it.

The people asked, "What should we do?"

"Turn away from your sins. Be baptized in the name of Jesus Christ," Peter answered. "Then your sins will be forgiven. You will receive the gift of the Holy Spirit."

So 3,000 people became believers! It was just the beginning. Word spread and each day more believed. The

believers studied what the disciples taught. People couldn't get enough of Jesus' amazing story! They shared everything they had. Every day they met in the temple to worship God and pray. Their hearts were glad and honest and true. People respected them. And God daily added others to the church.

God used the disciples to do miracles and wonders, and to heal people. God hadn't left them when Jesus returned to heaven. As Jesus promised, God was still with them, working through the Holy Spirit.

The disciples were changed men. They declared the truth fearlessly—even when people tried to stop them or hurt them. And more and more people became believers.

Questions:

1. How do you think the wind might have sounded? What would the tongues of fire look like?
2. After Peter's sermon, the new believers met together and learned about Jesus. This is how the church began. What do you learn about Jesus at church?

Prayer:

Thank God for sending His Spirit to live in you and for church.

A Coward No More

(Acts 3:1–4:31; 5:12–16; 9:32–11:18; 12:1–19)

"Spare coins?" Peter and John stopped, causing a stream of people heading into the temple for afternoon prayer to pass around them. Nearby a beggar sat on a dirty pile of rags in the shade of the Beautiful Gate, his legs twisted and shriveled.

"Come on, John!" Peter said, threading his way to the beggar. The man looked up, expecting money. "I don't have silver or gold," Peter said. "But I'll give you what I have." The beggar no longer seemed interested, pushing his cup toward others passing by.

"In the name of Jesus Christ of Nazareth, get up and walk." Peter commanded, taking the man's hand and pulling him up. Right away the beggar's ankles and feet untwisted and his legs grew muscle. The beggar stared, open-mouthed, then jumped, then YELLED! Praising God, he ran into the temple. People recognized him. He'd been begging at the temple for years. They gathered around Peter, waiting for some explanation.

"Faith in Jesus has healed him," Peter said, quick to grab the chance to preach. He told the crowd about Jesus and how He rose from the dead. Many who heard his message believed.

The religious rulers were very displeased and arrested Peter and John the next day. "Never speak to anyone in Jesus' name," they ordered.

"Should we obey you? Or God?" Peter asked. "We have to speak about the things we've seen and heard." The leaders warned them again, and then let them go.

God worked many other miracles through Peter. Some were even healed when Peter's shadow touched them!

In time, Peter left Jerusalem to teach believers in other towns. One day in Joppa, Peter rested on the flat roof of Simon the tanner. A welcome breeze blew away the dreadful stink of tanning. Suddenly, Peter saw something like a large sheet being lowered from heaven. It was filled with creatures God had told Jews not to eat.

God said, "Get up, Peter. Kill and eat."

"No, Lord! I will not!" Peter replied, "I have never eaten anything that is not pure and 'clean.'"

"Do not say anything is not pure that God has made

'clean,'" the voice answered.

This happened three times before the sheet was taken back up to heaven. Peter was trying to understand what this meant when the Holy Spirit spoke to him. "Simon, three men are looking for you. Get up and go downstairs. Don't let anything keep you from going with them. I have sent them."

Peter went downstairs to find the men at Simon's door. They weren't Jews, and they wanted Peter to come to the house of a Roman named Cornelius. Jews considered non-Jews unclean. But now Peter knew God wanted him to go.

Cornelius loved God. "An angel told me to send for you," he explained. "We're ready to hear what God wants you to tell us." He'd gathered his family and friends to listen.

Peter began telling them about Jesus. Even before he'd finished, the Holy Spirit came on everyone who heard him—just as He'd come on the believers at Pentecost. Peter took the happy news to Jerusalem: Forgiveness of sins and eternal life was for everyone. God would make anyone clean who asked!

The church continued to grow peacefully for about 13 years. Then a new King Herod arrested some disciples. He had James, John's brother, killed. The Jewish leaders were so pleased that Herod decided to arrest Peter, too, and threw him into prison.

Peter was ready to die for Jesus, if necessary. At peace,

he stretched out on the stale, filthy straw and *slept*. He wasn't worried—God was in control. There were two soldiers chained to Peter's wrists. Two more guarded the door. Suddenly an angel appeared and bright light filled the stone-walled cell. "Quick, get up!" he said. The cold chains fell off Peter's wrists and he rose, sleepily. "Put on your clothes and sandals," the angel told him. "Follow me."

Peter thought he was dreaming. The angel led him out of prison right past the guards. And the iron city gate opened by itself. Then the angel disappeared. Peter was free!

For another twenty years Peter traveled, teaching others about Jesus. His letters helped Christians to grow and to handle persecution. Just as Jesus had commanded him, Peter spent his life "feeding God's sheep."

Questions:

1. What would it be like to see a vision like Peter did?
2. Peter changed from being afraid and denying Jesus to being bold for Jesus. How can you be bold?

Prayer:

Thank God for loving you and working in you. Ask Him to help you grow and, like Peter, help others.

Persecutor Turned Missionary

(Acts 6:8–8:3; 9:1–31; 11:19–30; 13:1–4)

Saul was furious! He watched the angry mob drag Stephen outside the city and throw him to the ground. Then they picked up stones to throw at Stephen because he was preaching for Christ. Serves him right, Saul thought. *Stephen called Jesus "Lord" and thought He forgave sins. Only God could do that!*

The Way of Jesus the believers taught went against everything Saul believed in. Saul was determined to destroy the church. Going from house to house in Jerusalem, he found believers and took them to prison. But believers scattered and took their teaching with them. The more Saul raged, the further the church spread!

"Now some of Jesus' followers are even in Damascus," Saul informed the high priest. "Roads lead everywhere from that city. Their lies will spread through the whole empire!" Saul scowled, then continued. "Give me letters to the synagogues in Damascus," he said. "I'll go arrest followers of the Way and bring them back."

So Saul set off with some friends for the six day journey by foot. It was hot and dusty as they trudged through dry, rolling hills. They could just see the walls of Damascus in the distance when a dazzling light suddenly shone all around them. Saul fell to the ground, stunned. He was terrified and closed his eyes, certain he had seen a Man in the light.

"Saul! Saul!" a voice demanded. "Why are you opposing Me?"

Shaking in fear, Saul asked, "Who are You, Lord?"

"I am Jesus. I am the One you are opposing. Now get up and go into the city. There you will be told what you must do." Then Saul opened his eyes, but still saw nothing. "I'm blind!" he cried.

Saul's friends had heard a noise while Saul was on the ground, but saw no one. They were shocked when Saul told them what had happened. Had *they* been fighting against the *Messiah*? Were Jesus' followers right? Confused, they rounded up the donkeys, helped Saul mount, and led him into Damascus.

For three days, Saul remained blind. He refused food and water, but stayed in his room to pray and think

through what had happened. *How could Jesus be the Messiah?* he asked himself over and over. He shuddered to think that he had been trying to stop God's work!

But God had a plan for Saul's life. He told a believer in Damascus named Ananias, "Go to the house. . .on Straight Street. Ask for a man from Tarsus named Saul. . . .I have chosen this man to work for Me. He will bring My name to those who aren't Jews and to their kings. He will bring My name to the people of Israel. I will show him how much he must suffer for Me."

Ananias knew Saul was the one who had been hurting the believers in Jerusalem. But he also knew that God had told him to go and pray for the man. So Ananias pushed through the hot streets until he reached the house. Taking a deep breath, he knocked.

Saul heard the knock and waited, unsure about what might happen to him next. Soon Ananias came into the room and placed his hands on Saul's head. "Brother Saul," he said, "you saw the Lord Jesus. . . .He has sent me so that you will be able to see again. You will be filled with the Holy Spirit."

Right away, something like scales fell from Saul's eyes. "I can see again!" he cried, looking up into Ananias' kind face. When Ananias told Saul what God had said, Saul wasted no time. Right away, he was baptized in water.

Saul started telling everyone what had happened. But the change in his life proved even more that Jesus really was the Christ. Only God could change a man's

heart and mind so quickly.

Later, when Saul returned to Jerusalem, many believers were still afraid of him. After all, he had been sending believers to prison before he went to Damascus. Maybe this was a trick. But a believer named Barnabas realized Saul was truthful. He took Saul to the disciples and introduced him—as a believer in Christ! When Saul began to preach boldly for Jesus, it soon became clear to everyone that this was the work God had planned for him from the beginning of time.

Questions:

1. What's your favorite part of this story? Why?
2. Saul called himself the worst of sinners. Jesus forgave him. Can you imagine anything Jesus would not forgive? Why or why not?

Prayer:

Thank God that the good news of Jesus is for everyone, including you, and that He forgives your sins when you ask Him to.

Paul: The First Church Planter

(Acts 13:1–15, 42–52; 14:1–20; 16:1–5, 16–34; 18:1–18; Romans 5:20–21; 1 Corinthians 13:1–13)

Priscilla thumped the dough one last time, then put the bread in the clay oven to bake. She wanted everything perfect. *I love having people come to my home,* she thought happily, as she gathered wildflowers into a vase.

Her husband Aquila had come from his workshop at lunchtime, trailing wood shavings and thread. "Someone came by this morning and offered to work for me. I sure could use the help. My tent building business is growing faster than I can manage."

Priscilla kissed Aquila's cheek as she brought his lunch. "Is it someone I'd know?"

"No," Aquila answered. "He's just arrived from Athens. It sounds as if he travels a lot. He's gone to get his tools, but I want to invite him to dinner, okay?"

"Of course," Priscilla answered. "We've plenty of food. And I know what it's like to be new in town." Priscilla and Aquila hadn't been in Corinth long themselves. They'd lived in Rome for many years, until the Emperor Claudius drove out all the Jews.

At day's end, Priscilla peeked out her window to catch a glimpse of their guest following Aquila from his workshop. *He's not very tall, but he walks proudly*, she thought. Dropping back the colorful curtain, she ran to the door.

"Priscilla, this is Paul," Aquila said, ushering in the man. Paul's brilliant eyes sparkled out of his lined and weathered face. Pricilla liked him at once.

As they ate, Paul described his travels and how he'd started many churches. But as the evening wore on, he began sharing how he'd met the risen Jesus on the road to Damascas, how he'd been blinded, and now had a new name. "Before that, I'd wanted to destroy His church," he explained.

Tears streamed down the couple's faces as Paul told them about his changed life and his love for the Jesus he'd once hated. This was what they'd been looking for all their lives.

"But I don't think you'll have much luck starting a church in Corinth," Priscilla said later. "It's a sinful city, filled with temples to false gods."

"That's exactly why I've come here," Paul replied. "Wherever there's a lot of sin, God's power is even stronger."

"Stay in our home then," Priscilla insisted, "at least until you find another place." So Paul stayed for one week, then two weeks, three weeks, four weeks...

Every Sabbath, Paul went to the synagogue, trying to get both Jews and Greeks to believe in Jesus. But when the Jews began to treat him badly, Paul left the synagogue and taught at the house of Titius Justus, a believer. Many Corinthians who heard Paul believed and were baptized.

Soon, Priscilla's and Aquila's home became a gathering place for new Christians. Everyone felt welcome there. And the couple grew strong in faith, able to answer many of the others' questions.

Paul stayed with Priscilla and Aquila for a year and a half, teaching the believers in Corinth how God wanted them to live. Finally, Paul said it was time for him to leave. "Take us with you," the couple pleaded. "We can help." So when Paul sailed for Syria, they were on the boat with him!

Paul stayed in touch with the Corinthian church, writing them letters to help solve problems and answer questions. Once, Paul learned that some people thought they were better than others and were putting people down. Paul wrote to them that the most important thing of all is love. "Love is patient. Love is kind. It does not

want what belongs to others. It does not brag. It is not proud. It is not rude. It does not look out for its own interests. It does not easily become angry. It does not keep track of other people's wrongs. Love is not happy with evil. But it is full of joy when the truth is spoken. It always protects. It always trusts. It always hopes. It never gives up."

Paul's letter helped the Corinthians get back on the right track. Paul wrote many other letters full of God's wisdom to churches he'd started. We can still read them today in the Bible.

Questions:

1. What does "Love is not happy with evil" mean?
2. Paul said it's important to cooperate and love one another. How can you do that?

Prayer:

Ask for God's help to learn from Paul's letters and to use your talents and gifts helping others.

Chained, but Not Ashamed

(Acts 21:27–36; 22:30–23:35; 25:1–12, 23–26:2; 27:1–28:31; Romans 1:16; Philippians 1:20; 2:2–5; 4:4–8; 2 Timothy 2:9; 1:7)

An angry crowd covered the temple steps in Jerusalem. Roman soldiers marched in, driving them back with the flat of their swords. At the center, covered in bruises, a man lay curled into a protective ball: Paul. As usual, the riot was about religion and Paul's preaching that Jesus had risen from the dead.

The soldiers arrested Paul, bound him in chains, and took him into the fort to get him away from the screaming crowd. "Kill him!" they shouted. "He isn't fit to live!"

Despite the angry riot, Paul was at peace as they took him away. *God's with me*, he thought. *I'm ready to die for Him if I need to.* In years of travel, Paul had made many enemies because of his powerful preaching. But through floggings, shipwrecks, robberies, hunger, floods—and more—God always had looked after him. Paul smiled, remembering how once God even rescued him from jail by an earthquake!

A prophet had warned Paul that he'd be arrested in Jerusalem. Now God spoke to his heart. "Be brave! You've told people about Me in Jerusalem. You'll do the same in Rome." As Paul thought about this in his room at the fort, a soldier showed his nephew in.

"Uncle," the young man gasped, eyes huge, "forty men have vowed not to eat or drink until you're dead!" His voice cracked. "I heard them plotting! When the commander takes you to the Jewish leaders, they'll kill you on the way."

"Tell the Roman commander what you've told me," Paul said calmly. The commanding officer wasn't about to put Paul, a Roman citizen, in danger. So he gathered 200 soldiers, 70 horsemen, and 200 men with spears to escort Paul out of Jerusalem to Governor Felix for safety. God wasn't done with Paul yet!

In Caesarea, people argued for two years about what to do with Paul. But he got to tell the governor and many others about Jesus! Paul didn't stop caring for his churches, either. He wrote them from prison: "Don't be proud. Be patient with one another. Stop lying and speak the truth in love. Watch your language, saying only what will help people. Forgive each other because Christ forgave you. And be thankful."

When Festus became the new governor, Paul told

him and the Jewish King Agrippa about Jesus too. As God had promised through Ananias thirty years before, Paul preached to rulers and kings. But he was still in prison. And God had said he would tell others about Jesus in Rome. Finally, Festus agreed to send Paul to appeal to Caesar, in Rome.

It was winter, a bad time to sail. Paul warned the captain and crew: "The ship and everything in it will be lost. Our own lives will be in danger also." But the commander didn't listen to what Paul said.

Sure enough, they got into trouble. A hurricane force wind blew them away from the coast and out to sea. For days, they tried to outrun the storm, throwing off cargo and equipment. Hopeless, the sailors refused to eat. Two weeks into the storm, Paul said, "I belong to God and serve Him. Last night His angel stood beside me. The angel said, 'Do not be afraid, Paul. You must go on trial in front of Caesar. God has show His grace by sparing the lives of all those sailing with you.'" Then he urged the sailors to eat and regain their strength.

Soon the roar of waves breaking on rocks told them they neared land. Aiming for a beach barely visible through the rain, they ran aground. Waves pounded the ship, breaking it apart. People scrambled to shore, swimming or floating on wreckage. But everyone escaped!

Months later, Paul arrived in Rome. He lived in a house and took care of himself, but he was always under guard. Many of his guards became Christians!

Paul refused to be discouraged. Instead, he used this

time to teach the churches about courage and faithfulness in difficult times. He wrote to Timothy, "I've even been put in chains like someone who has committed a crime. But God's word is not held back by chains!" And to the Romans he wrote, "I am not ashamed of the good news of Jesus' death and resurrection. It's God's power and will save everyone who believes."

"Make my joy complete by agreeing with one another. Have the same love," he wrote to the church in Philippi. And "Don't worry about anything, instead tell God about everything. . . .Then God's peace will watch over your hearts and your minds. . . .Follow my example."

No matter what happened to him, Paul loved and worked for God. He taught people how to follow Jesus, just as he did himself.

Questions:

1. Why do you think Paul was so sure everyone would be saved during the shipwreck?
2. Which of the things that Paul wrote to Christians is something you can remember to do?

Prayer:

Ask God's help to live the way He wants you to and obey what He told Paul to write.

John, the Beloved Disciple

(John 13:23–25; 14:15–24;
15:9, 12–17; 19:25–27;
20:2–8; 21:7, 20–25; 1 John 1:9;
2:5, 10–11; 3:1–2, 16–18; 4:7–21)

John stretched to get the kinks out of his back as he rolled out of bed. He was getting old. He looked out his window at the rocky ground, sparse grass, and scrubby trees. Patmos! The tiny island prison where the Romans put people they wanted out of the way. *It's a far cry from the lush hillsides of Galilee,* John thought. Since the Romans couldn't get John to stop preaching and "disturbing the peace," they'd sent him here. It was a place people easily forgot—and where you were easily forgotten.

John smiled. No matter where they sent him, God would never forget him! Nor could he forget. It was very lonely here, away from the churches and other Christians.

Memories flooded through him. *At least I have a lot of time to think,* he grinned to himself.

John remembered the day Jesus called him and his brother James. Right away they'd dropped their dad's fishing nets to follow Him! *I was so blessed,* John thought. *Peter, James, and I went everywhere with Him, even to places the other disciples couldn't. Back then I thought I should get special treatment, be first in God's kingdom.* John gazed at the Mediterranean Sea in the distance, blushing even now at his own selfishness.

At their last meal together, John had laid his head against Jesus' chest, feeling safe and special. Knowing that He would soon die, Jesus kept teaching His disciples that night. "I will ask the Father. And He will give you another Friend to help you and to be with you forever. The Friend is the Spirit of truth. . . .He lives with you and He will be in you."

"I will not leave you like children who don't have parents," Jesus said. "I will come to you.

"Anyone who has My commands and obeys them loves Me. My Father will love the one who loves Me. I too will love him. And I will show myself to him."

Over and over, Jesus had said, "This is My command: Love one another." *That's when I really began to understand that everyone in the kingdom is special to God,* John thought.

John pictured the empty tomb as he found it that first morning. What joy! *Jesus is alive!* He'd never really

left. The Holy Spirit had come to be with them—with us—and was even on this lonely island, loving him. *God is love*, John whispered aloud. *So, we should love and show it by obeying God and loving others.*

Love. John had spent his whole life doing his best to follow Jesus' example. Love and forgiveness filled his letters to the churches in Asia. "God is faithful and fair," he wrote. "If we admit that we have sinned. . . . He will forgive every wrong thing we have done. He will make us pure."

"How great is the love the Father has given us so freely! Now we can be called children of God. And that's what we really are," John wrote another time. "We know what love is because Jesus Christ gave His life for us. . . . Don't just talk about love. Put your love into action."

Smiling at the picture of a church full of God's love, John drifted off to sleep. Another day of exile on Patmos, filled by the presence of God.

The next morning, John prayed as he walked slowly along the island's shore. God's Spirit filled him. Suddenly he heard a voice like rushing water behind him say, "Write on a scroll what you see." As John turned to see who had spoken, Jesus stood before him in a vision. His face was like the sun shining in all of its brightness! John fell at His feet, shaking.

"Do not be afraid," Jesus said, touching John on the shoulder. "I am the First and Last. I am the Living One. I was dead. But look! I am alive for ever and ever! And I hold the keys to Death and Hell. So write down what

you have seen. Write about what is happening now and what will happen later."

That day, John saw in his vision what would happen at the end of everything. He wrote it all down and saved it so we could read it too.

In time, the Romans allowed John to leave Patmos and return to Ephesus. Just as he'd planned, John taught and guided the church in Jesus' clear message: "For God loved the world so much that He gave His only Son so that anyone who believes in Him won't die but live forever."

John lived longer than all the other disciples and taught this message his whole life.

Questions:

1. If you were going to write a book about Jesus, what would you talk about?
2. What ways can you think of that God has shown you His love?

Prayer:

Ask for God's help to understand how much He loves you, and to help you to love others.

God's Kingdom

(Matthew 24:14; Acts 1:6–8; 1 Thessalonians 4:16–5:2; Revelation 12:1–17; 21:1–7; 22:20)

You've almost reached the end of the book—and the story of God's plan! From the beginning of time, God wanted children He could love who would love Him back: people He could teach, spend time with, and fill with happiness. Adam and Eve messed everything up for us all when they disobeyed God. But God had a plan to make us His children again: He promised Adam and Eve that one day their Son would crush Satan's head and Satan would crush His heel. God meant that one day the woman's descendant would be wounded, but he would destroy God's enemy.

For thousands of years God worked on His plan.

He made Abraham's family into the nation of Israel. He chose the tribe of Judah, and then David's family, and promised David his descendent would rule forever as king.

God also wanted His people to live the best way, so He gave Moses and other prophets His commands. But did His people obey? No! Like Adam and Eve, they turned away from God. God warned them over and over what would happen if they didn't follow Him. When they kept sinning, He let them be taken away from their promised land. But He still loved them and wanted them to know His plan, so in time He brought them home. Finally, they tried to do things His way!

When everything was ready, God chose Mary, David's descendent, to fulfill His promise to Adam and Eve. He gave her His own Son. Jesus never once disobeyed God or chose His own way. God let Satan "crush His heel" by killing Jesus on the cross. Jesus died for our sins. But He rose again, "crushing Satan's head," defeating him!

God wanted everyone in the world, not just the Jews, as His children. So He sent His Holy Spirit to help people to take the good news everywhere. Now we can be God's children! We can be forgiven and have a wonderful relationship with God. His plan worked!

The Jews had thought God's promise to David meant an ordinary kingdom. They waited for hundreds of years for God to set it up. After Jesus rose again, His disciples still asked if He'd defeat the Romans and set up a

kingdom for Israel like David's—only better. But that's not what God meant.

Jesus told them that they shouldn't be concerned about times or dates. Their job was to tell people about Him and spread His kingdom. Jesus meant that God's kingdom is spiritual—God ruling in people's hearts. After Jesus returned to heaven right before the disciples' eyes, angels promised that He would come back just as they'd seen Him leave. So Jesus' followers have been waiting for His return ever since. When He comes, He'll set up His kingdom on earth, as well as in people's hearts.

Near the end of the apostle John's life, on the island of Patmos, God gave him visions that tell how God and His people completely defeat Satan in the end. Satan tries to destroy God's Church and make His people turn away from Him. But God's true followers will stay faithful, and God protects them.

God told John that then He will make a new heaven and a new earth. He will make His home with people. They will be His people and He will be their God. He will wipe away every tear from their eyes. There will be no more death or sadness. There will be no more crying or pain. It will be God's special kingdom, a perfect place where He rules with love and kindness and everyone loves and obeys Him as their Father. He will have the children that He wanted from the beginning, to spend time with, teach, and fill with happiness!

When will this happen? No one knows. But Jesus said, "This good news of the kingdom will be preached in the whole world. It will be a witness to all nations. Then the end will come."

Our job is to keep loving and obeying God, and to spread His kingdom by helping everyone know about Him. One day, there'll be a loud shout and trumpet blast. God's children will be taken up in the clouds to meet Jesus in the air. We'll be with Him forever in His kingdom! Now *that's* something to look forward to!

Questions:

1. When you think of heaven, what do you hope it will be like for you?
2. What are some ways you can help get the message of Jesus preached to the whole world?

Prayer:

Thank God for giving you the Bible so you can learn about Him. Pray that everyone can hear about Jesus so He can come back soon.

Welcome to the Family!

Heritage
Builders®

Helping You Build a Family of Faith

We hope you've enjoyed this book. Heritage Builders was founded in 1995
by three fathers with a passion for the next generation. As a new ministry of
Focus on the Family, Heritage Builders strives to equip, train, and motivate
parents to become intentional about building a strong spiritual heritage.

It's quite a challenge for busy parents to find ways to build a spiritual foundation
for their families—especially in a way they enjoy and understand.
Through activities and participation, children can learn biblical truth
in a way they can understand, enjoy—and *remember.*

Passing along a heritage of Christian faith to your family is a parent's highest
calling. Heritage Builders' goal is to encourage and empower you in this
great mission with practical resources and inspiring ideas that really work—
and help your children develop a lasting love for God.

* * *

How To Reach Us

For more information, visit our Heritage Builders Web site! Log on to
www.heritagebuilders.com to discover new resources, sample activities, and ideas to help
you pass on a spiritual heritage. To request any of these resources, simply call Focus on
the Family at 1-800-A-FAMILY (1-800-232-6459) or in Canada, call 1-800-661-9800.
Or send your request to Focus on the Family, Colorado Springs, CO 80995. In Canada,
write Focus on the Family, P.O. Box 9800, Stn. Terminal, Vancouver, B.C. V6B 4G3

To learn more about Focus on the Family or to find out if there is an
associate office in your country, please visit www.family.org

We'd love to hear from you!

LIGHTWAVE
building Christian faith in families

Lightwave Publishing is one of North America's leading developers of quality resources that encourage, assist, and equip parents to build Christian faith in their families. Their products help parents answer their children's questions about the Christian faith, teach them how to make church, Sunday school, and Bible reading more meaningful for their children, provide them with pointers on teaching their children to pray, and much, much more.

Lightwave, together with its various publishing and ministry partners, such as Focus on the Family, has been successfully producing innovative books, music, and games since 1984. Some of their more recent products include *God's Great News for Children, A Parents' Guide to the Spiritual Growth of Children, Joy Ride!, Mealtime Moments,* and *My Time With God.*

Lightwave also has a fun kids' Web site and an Internet based newsletter called Tips and Tools for Spiritual Parenting. For more information and a complete list of Lightwave products, please visit: **www.lightwavepublishing.com.**